ENDURANCE EXPERTS

A Perspective on Suffering
from an Eastern Millennial
Living in the West.

KENNY DAMARA

WIPF & STOCK · Eugene, Oregon

ENDURANCE EXPERTS
A Perspective on Suffering from an Eastern Millennial Living in the West

Copyright © 2018 Kenny Damara. All rights reserved. Except for brief quotations in critical publications or reviews, no part of this book may be reproduced in any manner without prior written permission from the publisher. Write: Permissions, Wipf and Stock Publishers, 199 W. 8th Ave., Suite 3, Eugene, OR 97401.

Wipf & Stock
An Imprint of Wipf and Stock Publishers
199 W. 8th Ave., Suite 3
Eugene, OR 97401

www.wipfandstock.com

PAPERBACK ISBN: 978-1-5326-7573-7
HARDCOVER ISBN: 978-1-5326-7574-4
EBOOK ISBN: 978-1-5326-7575-1

Manufactured in the U.S.A.   12/18/18

Unless indicated, all scripture quotations taken from the New American standard Bible®, Copyright © 1960, 1962, 1963, 1968, 1971, 1972, 1973, 1975, 1977, 1995 by The Lockman Foundation. Used by permission. (www.Lockman.org)

Where NKJV is indicated scripture taken from the New King James Version®. Copyright © 1982 by Thomas Nelson. Used by permission. All rights reserved.

Scripture quotations marked (NLT) are taken from the Holy Bible, New Living Translation, copyright ©1996, 2004, 2015 by Tyndale House Foundation. Used by permission of Tyndale House Publishers, Inc., Carol Stream, Illinois 60188. All rights reserved.

*To my brothers and sisters at The Moody Church,
who endure.*

Contents

Acknowledgments | ix
Introduction | xi

Chapter 1
Suffering and Salvation in Circles | 1

Chapter 2
Breaking the Circle: The Suffering Soul before God | 10

Chapter 3
Coming Full Circle: East or West, this World is not Heaven | 23

Chapter 4
The Response to Suffering: The Gigantic Secret of the Christian | 34

Chapter 5
The Reasons for Suffering | 47

Chapter 6
The Rewards for Suffering Well | 63

Chapter 7
The End of Suffering: When East and West Converge | 81

Epilogue
When God Gives Out the Medals | 97

Bibliography | 99

Acknowledgments

I WISH TO THANK Jennifer Millard, Tim Larsen, Steve Mason, Michaela Novakovic, and Nathaniel Hodson for your invaluable input in reviewing the manuscript. I thank Aimee Lilly, for lending your skill and excellence to the process of editing. Thanks also to Charles Brown III, Phil Zahn, and Adi Selfollari, for your prayers and encouragement along the way, which have made this project a reality. Thank you, Bryan Butler, for your creative artwork on the cover. Thank you, Thomas Jacob, for your hard work in marketing. I thank the team at Wipf and Stock for your wonderful cooperation and flexibility in allowing this book to be published in a timely manner. Thanks to the many other friends and family who have prayed for the writing and success of this book. My deepest gratitude and thanks, however, goes to the Lord Jesus Christ—You who have overseen my experience and articulation of this topic by Your sovereign and loving hand.

Introduction

EVERY YEAR IN CHICAGO, just around the time fall is coming into its fullness, thousands of runners participate in a feat of endurance called the Chicago Marathon. These runners hail from various parts of the United States and the world. A few times I have had the opportunity to stand on the sidelines to watch and cheer these runners as they pass by, flint-faced, having just one goal in mind: beginning mile 1, and finishing mile 26.2. What goes on between these mile markers is endurance. When they have crossed the finish line, every runner gets a medal, a tangible recognition that they have endured and finished the race.

When God Gives Out the Medals

Eric Liddell, perhaps most well-known for winning the 400-meter gold in the 1924 Paris Olympics, refused to run his specialty, the 100-meter race, because it was on a Sunday. Since Liddell, a devout Christian, wanted to honor God by attending church on Sundays, he chose instead to run the 400-meter race which was on a weekday. Against all odds, he went on to shock the world by not only winning the race, but by setting a new world record of 47.6 seconds—making him a national hero back home in Scotland. At one celebration dinner honoring their champ, Liddell spoke, displaying more maturity than one would expect from a twenty-two-year-old:

> "It has been wonderful to compete in the Olympic Games and to bring home a gold medal. But since I have been a young lad, I have had my eyes on a different prize. You see, each of us is in a greater race than any I have run in Paris, and this race ends when God gives out the medals."[1]

---

1. Benge, *Eric Liddell*, 69.

Introduction

In the "greater race" that Liddell refers to—the marathon of life, with its accompanying suffering—we can never respond rightly without instruction on endurance from God and his Word, the Bible. Liddell's attitude toward running was a reflection of his attitude toward life. He ran not only to endure the rigors of Olympic races, but also the race of life. He was not satisfied with merely winning Olympic gold. His post-Olympic life proved that Liddell would willingly endure suffering in order to win eternal gold.

After the glitz and glory of the Olympics faded away, Liddell would be exposed to the hardships of Christian missions in Tientsin, China. As a missionary, Eric Liddell—the hero of Scotland— would suffer hunger, injury, sleeping on cold dirt floors, sickness, separation from family, theft, violence, and finally an untimely death in an internment camp under the cruel hands of the Japanese army as they ravaged China in the early and mid-1940s.

Eric Liddell endured suffering, having learned figuratively as a track runner what it means to endure suffering on the longer track of life. His endurance in life was as unmistakable as his endurance on the track. A friend who observed Eric in his suffering said of him, "I never saw Eric angry. I never heard him say a cross or unkind word. He just went about doing good."[2] Although Liddell competed in short-distance races on the track, when it came to suffering in the race of life, he was a marathon runner.

Becoming an Endurance Expert

In order to finish a marathon, a runner must endure hardship both before and during the race. Before the race they endure all the rigors of training. During the race they endure sweat, thirst, fatigue, muscle pains, sometimes a lack of motivation, and change in terrain and gradient. Those who run to finish the race endure. What's most important is that they are able to successfully run the marathon only because they have trained for it; they have grown, by degrees, to a stage where they can indeed endure to finish the race. By the time the race day comes, they have become "endurance experts," so to speak, in marathon running.

For the Christian, rightly responding to suffering can be likened to successfully enduring the rigors of training for and running a marathon. Why does this apply specifically to Christians?

---

2. Benge, *Eric Liddell*, 166.

Introduction

Well, firstly, to receive the medal from God for endurance, one must know God through his Son Jesus Christ. This is the first step, just as one must first register with the organizers of the Chicago Marathon to participate in the race. One can't just jump in to the Chicago Marathon at any time! Try, and authorities may pull you from the race! Besides all the training before the race, you must have your name registered with the organizers, be given a marathon bib with your number on it, and then run to receive a medal at the end of the race. Similarly, only when your name is registered with God, written in Heaven in the book of life—only when you have believed on God's Son Jesus Christ and received the new life he imparts—does he supply all you need to endure the suffering in your life. God ensures that you will endure. Not just anyone can respond to suffering in the ways that will be explored and explained in this book. Not just anyone can begin the journey to becoming an endurance expert. You must first come to Christ, who endured suffering; you must learn from him, and then you will be on your way to becoming an endurance expert.

Perhaps you have not yet come to Christ, and you are contemplating your own suffering as you read this. Perhaps this is the time when the voice of Christ calls to you. When you receive him as your Savior, he will give you meaning in your suffering, in light of his suffering.

A Disclaimer

Now, just in case you are offended by the title and concept of being an "endurance expert"— perhaps you think it's pompous of me to posit that someone can become an endurance "expert," or perhaps you think I'm saying I have attained this expertise and know how to respond to all the various sufferings of life in expert fashion—let me offer a disclaimer. Or maybe for you the phrase has an advertising slogan feel to it. Let me explain what I mean by it.

In a marathon, the status of "endurance expert" can be said to have been achieved only after one crosses the finish line, not before. So too, the Christian becomes an endurance expert (as I am defining it) having endured suffering rightly and having crossed the finish line of life into eternity, *"when God gives out the medals."*[3] I, Kenny Damara, have not crossed the finish line of life into eternity . . . so I am not an endurance expert. No one reading this book, or alive today, has crossed the finish line. So, neither

---

3. Benge, *Eric Liddell*, 69.

are you an endurance expert. Assuredly we are all at different places in how we have learned to react or respond to suffering—some able to better respond to suffering the way God desires—but none of us has arrived. This book then is not written by an expert, neither written to experts, but rather written as we journey toward *becoming* endurance experts.

Many people object to the idea of God's existence because of suffering, pain, and evil. There are some excellent books that that help us respond to those objections. My purpose in writing is not primarily to respond to those objections, although that may arise as part of what we explore. Rather, I write this book *to point you to the right response to suffering itself*, the response that is born out of the Christian, biblical viewpoint.

I write this book from the viewpoint of *an Eastern Millennial living in the West*. Hence the subtitle of the book. I hope to benefit a wide demographic of readers, but am also thinking specifically—please note—of *Millennials, both Christians and non-Christians,* who need hope in suffering. A lack of commitment is one of the maladies of the Millennial generation and is even more magnified in the marathon of suffering.

How Does This Apply Today?

In a culture that screams ease, convenience, and escape from suffering, how does training toward becoming an endurance expert apply?

Ours is a culture of *ignorance* when it comes to suffering. Most people, even many Christians, do not know *why* suffering exists. There is also ignorance about the current suffering of others. Who are those people undergoing untold suffering in the world right now and what is causing it? For example, Voice of the Martyrs regularly publishes statistics on the number of Christians worldwide who are suffering persecution[4] and those being held as prisoners.[5] How many of us know about the suffering of those being persecuted and imprisoned? More importantly, how many of us gauge our suffering in the light of their suffering? On the other hand, some of us, while being aware of the persecution of others, may gauge our own suffering as nonexistent in comparison to theirs, consequently remaining ignorant of how to respond.

Ours is also a culture of *escapism*. Eastern religions and mysticism have come to the West and consolidated the already universal human tendency

---

4. www.icommittopray.com, "Church Disbands Because of Hindu Persecution."
5. www.prisoneralert.com, "All Prisoners."

Introduction

to want to escape suffering instead of enduring it. Practices like Yoga and Transcendental Meditation have smuggled in with them an escapist outlook to life and suffering. Someone who leads this charge in the American media—someone whose influence you should be aware of—is Oprah Winfrey. She often instructs people on how to "live your best life."[6] Ironically, "televangelist" Joel Osteen, who misrepresents the Christian viewpoint on suffering, has written about how to have *Your Best Life Now*. The *zeitgeist* of escapism is prevalent both within and without the Church today.

Finally, ours is a culture of *illusion*. When you are ignorant about the truth and seek to escape reality, you end up living in an illusory bubble. As we work to change the outward condition of peoples' lives, we put our hope in that which deceives while we turn away from the truth that has the power to transform the human heart. For example, consider the UNO, or any Islamofascist group, or a dictatorial, communist government led by some tyrant. Consider the academia in our historic universities here in the U.S., which has been brainwashed by atheistic and naturalistic philosophy. To some extent, the common denominator in all these groups is a tireless striving toward a heaven on earth. But not just these groups. You and I are prone to the same while trying to chase the "American dream!" Striving to enter God's Heaven is ignored, while illusive utopias are sought.

In a culture of *ignorance, escapism,* and *illusion,* learning how to respond rightly to suffering is necessary. Also, in such a milieu, no endeavor can be more realistic—because suffering is an inescapable reality.

Join me, then, for this journey on becoming an endurance expert. It will be worth your time, because if you are not suffering now, or even if you have never suffered, you will suffer one day in some way. That is not my wish for you, but simply a fact in this broken and fallen world. My earnest prayer for you, therefore, is that this book will help you to respond rightly to suffering and to cross the finish line into eternity, *"when God gives out the medals."*

---

6. Winfrey, "What Oprah Knows for Sure."

Chapter 1

Suffering and Salvation in Circles

HAVE YOU EVER WATCHED a hamster on a running wheel? It runs inside a moving circle, seemingly with an immense sense of purpose, but gets nowhere. This is kind of hilarious to watch! Similarly—although it's not hilarious—living in ignorance about the right way to respond to suffering causes us to live like a hamster in the circle of a running wheel. In order to get somewhere, rather than going nowhere despite much movement, we need to know how to respond intellectually and experientially to questions such as, "Why does suffering exist? And how should I face suffering in my life and in the world around me?" These are questions we all ask during life's toughest moments.

People have always wondered why suffering exists and how we are to respond to it. Like many people today, Siddhartha Gautama—the ancient Indian prince who became the Buddha—also asked these questions. The life of the Buddha and his search for truth are a warning about the reality of suffering, the impact it can have on a person, and how to respond to this reality.

The Suffering of the Buddha

Historical accounts tell us that Siddhartha Gautama was born in Kapilavastu, near Nepal. Buddhist tradition has it that his father, King Suddhodana, wished to shield Siddhartha from the ills of life that were driving people of

Endurance Experts

his time to seek salvation through the rigorous means of asceticism.[1] Like many parents today, he had dreams of what he wanted his son to become. Suddhodana wanted Siddhartha to be a great king who would further their empire. Despite his father's efforts, Siddhartha did discover suffering when he ventured outside the protection and comfort of the palace.

As the story goes, Siddhartha's discovery of suffering was the result of three or four successive visits to Lumbini Park, where his attention was held by things that seemed abnormal to his princely eyes: a decrepit old man, a diseased man, a dead man, and finally an ascetic.[2]

On each of these trips he was accompanied by one of his servants, who gave him an explanation of the suffering Siddhartha saw. When at first Siddhartha came upon the old man, he was perplexed by the fact that humans grow old, and wondered if this would happen to him. He learned from his servant that all humans grow old and weak with time. On his next trip, he came upon a sick and dying man. This too shocked him, and he learned that humans fall prey to sickness and disease. On the third trip, the commotion of a man being carried to a funeral on a bier arrested his attention. His servant explained that the man was dead. He learned that all humans are born and must die one day. He was deeply disturbed by the reality of death.

The reality of suffering in its various hues shook Siddhartha to his soul . . . just as perhaps you, dear reader, are deeply disturbed by the reality of suffering in the world, and in your own life.

On yet another trip, Siddhartha saw a religiously-clad man, who had a serene expression on his face and seemed to have found spiritual victory. I am making a pure guess, but a highly plausible one, that having seen all this, Siddhartha probably asked, "What does one do with so much suffering in life, and how does one emerge victorious like this serene man?" At any rate, he did not know how to respond to all that he had seen, and so after these encounters, he began his search for the truth. He was determined to find the reason for suffering and the remedy for it.

Accounts relate how Siddhartha travelled to various teachers and sages, from whom he sought truth, only to be disappointed each time. Later he retired to the forest to seek truth on his own through severe discipline and meditation, so much so that at one point when "he touched the skin

---

1. Drummond, *Gautama the Buddha*, 32–3.
2. Drummond, *Gautama the Buddha*, 32–3.

of his belly, he took hold of his backbone."³ After six or seven years, when he realized that this extreme method brought him no peace or liberation, he resorted to the "Middle Way," a system with neither the rigors of meditation he was going through nor the normal pleasures other sages were permitting. One day he finally found "enlightenment" when he was sitting under the serenity of a large tree. So it is said that Siddhartha Gautama had become the Buddha, the enlightened one, the one who had conquered suffering and was able to affirm,

> I am freed; and I comprehended . . . ignorance was dispelled, knowledge arose, darkness was dispelled, light arose even as I abided diligent, ardent, self-resolute.⁴

The Buddha was born, or rather self-made: the one who, through the powers of his mind and heart, had supposedly escaped or overcome suffering in the flesh. Wouldn't many today give anything to escape or overcome suffering through this Middle Way philosophy? Sadly, many today, thinking it possible, have bitten into the worm of the Middle Way methodology—hook, line, and sinker!

Salvation in Circles

As I observe these events in the life of the Buddha, I can't help but notice that his quest for truth and salvation may have come full circle after all was said and done, so that in the end he arrived at no better conclusion than when he first began. There is something about Siddhartha Gautama's perception of salvation, and what it means to be saved or liberated, that makes me think he never arrived at the state of enlightenment he claimed—or that this "enlightened state" was actually one of even greater darkness and deception than when as a young prince he was shielded from the reality of suffering by his father. What he said on two significant occasions causes this suspicion in me. First, what he said upon supposedly being enlightened, and second, what he said on his deathbed.

At the time of his so-called enlightening, notice that he said, "I am freed . . ."⁵ Whenever a person claims to be free, it begs three questions. First, who or what are they free from? Second, what bound them to what

---

3. Drummond, *Gautama the Buddha*, 36–7.
4. Drummond, *Gautama the Buddha*, 38–9.
5. Drummond, *Gautama the Buddha*, 38–9.

they are now free from? And third, who freed them from what they could not resist being bound by? Please think about that sequence for a moment.

To answer these questions in the case of Siddhartha: He was freed from suffering; ignorance bound him; but then, who freed him? He answers this in the same quote above, "*I abided diligent, ardent, self-resolute.*"[6] Many years later, on his deathbed, he said, "All component things in the world are *changeable*. They are not *lasting. Work hard to gain your own salvation.*"[7] Or as another version records,

> The master opened his lips a last time, "*All things individual die—* strive earnestly—to find *liberation—*" his last faint words mingled and were lost in the breeze that stirred the sal trees.[8] (Emphasis mine)

Several things are conspicuous about Siddhartha's notion of salvation. First, it is something a person must gain for themselves by abiding "diligent, ardent, self-resolute." You must "work hard" to gain it, just as he did. But once you have gained it you still have no hope, because—in his own words—all things, including the one who has gained his own salvation, "die"; they are "changeable," and "not lasting." Where then has a person who has worked hard to earn his own salvation arrived, when at the end of his life he comes to die, and is trusting in that same hard work which is "changing" and "not lasting"? If the hard work is "not lasting," has he not arrived at the same point where he began his quest for salvation, to once again begin that hard work? Isn't this a circular notion of salvation? Hasn't the person gone around in circles time and time again, only to arrive again at the point where they began, of having no assurance of being saved or liberated?

This is what I'd like to call the doctrine of "Salvation in Circles." It is actually an oxymoron, because true salvation does not see people being led in circles, but ultimately liberates them with the truth from the circular rut of lies they are caught in, allowing them to progress onward. I call it Salvation in Circles only to illustrate the worldview it represents: that of believing one has been liberated in life, and then admitting the hopelessness of one's self-saving efforts when faced with the reality of death.

---

6. Drummond, *Gautama the Buddha*, 38–9.
7. Buddhanet, "Life of the Buddha (part 2)."
8. Byles, *Footprints of the Gautama Buddha*, 204–5.

Suffering and Salvation in Circles

As you read, I wonder if you see your life described here. In your quest for meaning and satisfaction, are you running around in circles looking for someone to save you?

By Salvation in Circles, I actually mean no salvation, no liberation, at all. It is present bondage, and if the circle is never straightened out, it ultimately leads to damnation; that is, to a future of eternal bondage. It may appear to be salvation or "nirvana" for the present but is only temporary escapism, which relegates you to a worse bondage than before once the escapade has run its course. In other words, at the end of life—whether people have skirted around suffering via the passing pleasure of hedonism, the rigors of what the Buddha proposed, or something in between—they will come to realize that their *escape was not permanent*, and they have never been fully and finally set free. What's worse, beyond death, they will realize that it is too late to make straight the path of salvation that was circular all through life. Indeed, beyond death, they will realize that they believed a lie in life, one that bound them for eternity.

Now some 2,500 years since its inception, you would think that this doctrine of Salvation in Circles would eventually be "straightened out" from within the ranks of Buddhism. Not so. Why does this circular notion of liberation continue to be believed, and in fact continue to grow in popularity among many so-called seekers of truth? Just a few years ago, an article in The Washington Post asked,

> Why is a faith founded under a Bodhi tree in India 2,500 years ago enjoying a newfound popularity in America today?[9]

Why indeed? In suggesting why, allow me to give you the *reason* for such a circular notion of salvation, and then give you the *result* this notion produces in the broader culture. In Chapter 6, I will "circle" back to consider *a sensible response* to the Salvation in Circles notion!

Salvation in Circles: The Reason

A circular notion of salvation continues to be believed all over the world, and has rapidly garnered popularity in America. Why? Mainly because in this notion, outside of self, you do not need a savior to be set free. Hear again the dying words of the Buddha: "*Work hard to gain your own salvation.*"[10]

9. Quinn, "What's an American Buddhist?"
10. Buddhanet, "Life of the Buddha (part 2)."

Self is both the one in need of being saved and at the same time the savior. Incredible! The very notion of liberation demands that you need someone superior to yourself to free you from that by which you could not resist being bound in the first place and from which you cannot save yourself now. For if you could save yourself, you wouldn't have succumbed to being bound by whatever or whoever you now struggle to be free from. Therefore, not being able to save ourselves, we need a Savior who can bend the circular road to nowhere into a straight and narrow road which leads to light and liberty. In fact, we need a Savior who can blaze a new road for us! We need a Savior who can assure us that we have truly been saved in this life, and that the salvation will last beyond this life. And when this life has come to an end, we need a Savior who will safely escort us from this world to our final destination—that time and place where all suffering will have ended.

But why do people *not* believe in such a Savior—one who is outside the self, and who can straighten the circle? In a few lines of poetry taken from his 1871 epic on the Buddha and Buddhism, Richard Phillips answer that question vicariously. He expresses the Buddha's views of truth and God:

> This will I do; for I have hope that now
> A way is opened. My heart says, 'Go thou
> And prosper, and do even as thou wilt
> To thy work. Thou shalt incur no guilt,
> Tho' teaching error and concealing truth;
> Because thou dost it from love and ruth,
> And these flow not from a polluted fount.
> There is no God to call thee to account.'[11]

The reason why people—the Buddha included—subscribe to a circular notion of salvation is because in this notion "there is no God to call thee to account." The reason why people don't see the necessity of having a savior outside of the self is because they see no God to call them to account. God calls human beings to account—he requires accountability to himself. Contrary to what the Buddha thought about God, the Bible says that it is God "to whom we must give account" (Hebrews 4:13). As people stuck in a circular notion of salvation, we hate accountability, and we love autonomy. Many Americans, Millennials in particular, need to be aware of the inconsistencies of these New Age and Eastern religious doctrines of liberty that have gripped our people, making us slaves to self rather than free from sin.

---

11. Phillips, *The Story of Gautama Buddha*, 128.

Suffering and Salvation in Circles

When you believe there is no God to call us to account, you run into big problems, even if you are the Buddha.

The first of these problems is this: who could question whether what the Buddha said was right or wrong? What standard did he give people to evaluate him by, if there was no God? None but a man-made standard, something he made up on his own! Secondly, if he told people no God exists, he was also telling them that they could never call into question the conclusions he arrived at. So as the one setting the standards for life, he was unwittingly setting himself up as a god—whether he said this or not—and expecting people to follow him.

Thirdly, once we believe there is no God to call us to account, we believe we can do whatever we wish—and indeed we do so—so long as we escape suffering and pursue pleasure. Isn't this what Phillips expressed of the Buddha in the poem? "My heart says, 'Go thou and prosper, and do even as thou wilt to thy work.'" Lastly, and most importantly, the non-existence of God precludes the existence of a worthy Savior outside the self—and so necessitates the creation of a savior inside the self, a self-savior, because now no one but self is seen as worthy or able to save.

Of course, these objections can be applied to other systems which are inconsistent with the truth. But to answer the question raised in the article from The Washington Post, these are the reasons why the faith founded under a Bodhi tree in India some 2,500 years ago is enjoying a newfound popularity in America today. In other words, at the heart of all reasons for ascribing to a Salvation in Circles ideology is the desire to have nothing to do with God—desiring autonomy instead of accountability. But there's more to Salvation in Circles—something I would like to dwell on briefly to further set the context for the rest of the book.

Salvation in Circles: The Result

The result of this circular notion of salvation (plus a no-God-to-call-thee-to-account attitude and a self-savior mentality) is a desire to escape the hard realities of existence and search for a perfect world of tranquility, where these hard realities do not exist and you feel nothing but bliss or total detachment. (I'm sorry to burst your Star Wars bubble here, but when Yoda says, "Train yourself to let go of everything you fear to lose," it is the coward's way out—a leaf out of the Buddha's book of working hard to gain your own salvation!) When you work to gain your own salvation, you begin travelling down a road—a highway—called escapism. On this highway the only thing you can think about is escaping the harsh *realities of this life* which you *do not want to understand*, and the even graver *reality of an afterlife* which you *cannot understand*. Now please read me rightly. I am not saying this about everyone who suffers, but particularly about people who follow the lead of the Buddha and other like-minded leaders, who "work hard to gain their own salvation" through suffering, and ultimately seek to escape suffering.

It is these people who "let go of everything" they fear to lose who then head down the road of escapism, which is supposed to lead to their utopia, elusive as it is. In other words, when you try to escape suffering rather than deal with it, you aren't going to go looking for worse circumstances, are you? Rather, having escaped suffering you will look for a place where suffering does not exist—a seemingly better place. On the road of escapism, you are travelling towards your utopia—a place that you imagine will once and for all rid you of every problem. So suffering is skirted, and a place some Easterners call "Shangri-La" is sought—a fictitious mystical paradise mentioned in the 1933 novel *Lost Horizon* by James Hilton.

There is only one problem in seeking this kind of Shangri-La.

Remember, the road of escapism is a circular road, and it never takes you to the Shangri-La or utopia it promises; instead it leaves you travelling in circles, because it cannot take you to a place that does not exist. Having no God in life leads to a circular notion of salvation, which is basically escapism. And escapism most often leads to utopianism. When that utopianism eventually fails and causes even more suffering, it all circles back, and you go looking for an escape route again. The hamster on the wheel keeps running, getting nowhere!

History has shown us many forms of utopianism: religious, social, political, emotional, and psychological. Time has proven them all to be failures. They leave us no better than before.

In the realm of religion, I have used the story of Siddhartha Gautama because it helps illustrate, both in word and deed, my point about Salvation in Circles. I have also used it because Buddhism represents a wrong response to suffering: escapism, which currently grips many people of the world—especially in Western nations like the United States, in which many are fascinated with Eastern mysticism. On a global scale, you find the United Nations trying to do the same thing in the social realm: pushing for world peace without being willing to pay the price for world peace—the price of suffering . . . for indeed no one in the UN is big enough to buy peace for the world.

In the political realm, we've seen people such as Hitler. Though he was labeled "anti-utopian" by some, he was essentially trying to create a time, place, and people who would fit his understanding of a perfect world: "a generation of young people devoid of conscience—imperious, relentless, and cruel."[12] In the psychological realm we have seen the likes of Freud, conjuring up theories of the mind to remedy the maladies of the human heart, without being able to first diagnose the condition. That too is tantamount to escapism.

Over time, all these efforts have tried to prescribe solutions to life's problems, without ever being able tell us what the problems are. In doing so, they have all ended up unwittingly instructing us on how to *escape* suffering. In all of these views, one is encouraged to seek some sort of heaven here on earth, where everything must be perfect. But lest you think I write to merely criticize worldviews other than Christianity, wait till Chapter 6 when I comment on certain so-called Christian camps that have an escapist outlook on life. Forms of escapism— albeit "Christianized"—have crept into the Church.

Suffering in today's world of connectivity and comfort is as real, vivid, and varied as it was in the days when the princely eyes of Siddhartha Gautama, the Buddha, beheld it. But what we need in today's politically correct and "tolerant of intolerance" society are not charlatan saviors who make empty promises and produce people who are escapist utopians. We need the Savior, Jesus Christ, who himself suffered to redeem people who would learn to endure suffering by trusting in him—people who would endure the reality of suffering on earth until he ushers them into the reality of Heaven.

But what are some practical responses even as we experience the urge to escape suffering and create little utopias of our own? It is these heartfelt yet practical responses to suffering that we turn to next.

---

12. Zacharias, *The End of Reason*, 51.

Chapter 2

Breaking the Circle: The Suffering Soul before God

> I said, "Oh, that I had wings like a dove!
> I would fly away and be at rest.
> Behold, I would wander far away,
> I would lodge in the wilderness. *Selah*.
> I would hasten to my place of refuge
> From the stormy wind and tempest."
> — Psalm 55:6–8

LISTEN WITH ME TO this heartfelt cry of King David, the writer of Psalm 55. Read these verses out loud and hear yourself saying them. Put yourself in the sandals of King David. Don't you often feel like this—like flying away to be at rest from all suffering, strife, and pain? This cry of David is the cry of untold millions today. It is the cry of everyone who has a body, a mind, a heart, a soul, a spirit. Anyone who does not echo this cry in some way or another, at some time in their life, is someone who is living in an illusory bubble of bliss and has so far successfully evaded or escaped suffering, denying themselves its privilege. Yes, suffering is a privilege—although it's difficult to admit.

To have never had the privilege of knowing what it is to suffer or to feel pain can be dangerous. I am thinking about people who suffer from a condition called *congenital insensitivity to pain*,[13] who cannot feel—and

---

13. Connor, "The People Who Can't Feel Pain."

never have felt—physical pain. They don't recognize when they are being injured, and so will do things like placing their hand on a hot stove without any realization that they are being severely burned. Professor Geoffrey Woods, who has researched the condition from the Cambridge Institute for Medical Research at Cambridge University, says this:

> The ability to sense pain is essential to our self-preservation, yet we understand far more about excessive pain than we do about lack of pain perception.[14]

There seems then to be a privilege in pain and suffering, in that it keeps us from influences—physical, emotional, and spiritual—that could kill us. Despite its positive effects, the majority of people who have had the privilege of suffering desire to be freed from it. It is a good thing to *desire* to be freed from suffering once and for all. It proves that we were made for eternal bliss, where no suffering is experienced. But while it is a good thing to desire to be freed from suffering, does *the desire* to be free grant us *the license* to engineer our own escapes? The answer, of course, can depend on the specific situation. For example, in the case of the suffering caused by an abusive spouse, it is certainly wise *to* escape. Or in the face of immediate physical danger, such as a burning building, we would be foolish *not* to engineer our own escape. Or in the case of the suffering brought on by a life-consuming addiction to recreational drugs, it would also be foolish *not* to escape the places or people that fuel this addiction. But to say that the desire to be free from *specific instances of suffering* grants us the license to engineer our own escapes from *all suffering in general*—that is, from the very presence of all suffering in this world—is a futile thing. It is futile because on this side of human existence, we cannot fully escape all suffering—as much as we may try. According to the Christian, biblical worldview, suffering is woven into the warp and woof of this fallen, broken world. (I will write more about this in Chapter 5.) Isn't this precisely what we see around us in our own experience? Even so, within the Christian, biblical framework there is still hope in a broken world.

If trying to escape all suffering is the wrong response, then there is a right response which leads to hope, both in specific sufferings that we should escape, and in suffering in general, which we wish to escape but would be better off enduring. The following is not *the* right response to

---

14. Connor, "The People Who Can't Feel Pain."

suffering, but an initial response that prepares us for the eventual and more enduring response in Chapter 4.

As we look at Psalm 55 and the historical situation in which it was written, we can see how King David responded to the specific suffering he wished to escape. His response is still very meaningful and applicable to us in this postmodern age, in which pain and suffering can be easily dismissed as meaningless by apathetic people such as Richard Dawkins. Dawkins says of suffering and pain in the world,

> . . . some people are going to get hurt, other people are going to get lucky, and you won't find any rhyme or reason in it, nor any justice.[15]

Is that his "scientific" explanation of suffering—so trite and simplistic? Far better for the so-called scientist to wish for wings to fly away from suffering! In Psalm 55, King David wrote that he wished for "wings like a dove" to fly away from his own suffering. Let's examine the situation in which he wrote this Psalm. It is especially interesting in contrast with what we just saw in the life of Siddhartha Gautama, another Eastern royal living before the time of Christ (400s or 300s B.C.). David lived in Jerusalem nearly 3,000 years ago (in the early 900s B.C.). In the biblical book of 2 Samuel, chapters 13–19 set the historical context in which he wrote the poetry of Psalm 55.

The Suffering of David

The account goes that David's son Absalom had murdered his half-brother Amnon—David's other son—in cold blood, because Amnon had raped Absalom's sister, Tamar, who was also Amnon's half-sister. After he murdered Amnon, Absalom fled and stayed away from home for three full years. During these three years David longed to see his son Absalom, despite the dark and lingering memory of his actions. When Absalom finally returned to Jerusalem, David did not see him for another two years. After five whole years, when David finally saw Absalom and kissed him in acceptance, Absalom turned traitorous and gradually began plotting against his father, stealing the hearts of David's people to himself. His plan was to stage a coup and take the kingdom from his father. After some years of this scheming, David finally caught wind of it; the tables turned, and David had to

---

15. Dawkins, *A River Out of Eden*, 133.

flee Jerusalem with his faithful men before Absalom could do them harm. To add insult to injury, David then learned that one of his most trusted advisers, his confidant and friend Ahithophel, had betrayed him and was a co-conspirator with Absalom.

Most of Israel was aware that a coup was underway, and that King David was on the run. As David and his men fled to the outskirts of Jerusalem, an old enemy named Shimei appeared out of the hills and began cursing David, hurling stones at the king and his camp as they traveled below him along the foothills. What's more, very shortly Absalom would lead the armies of Israel in an attempt to find David and his camp to kill them all.

Spare a thought for David here. A lot was happening that gave him the understandable desire to escape.

For David, this had to be the height of mental pressure, emotional anguish, physical fatigue, and spiritual struggle. He had been betrayed by his family (Absalom), his friend (Ahithophel), and his countrymen (those Israelites who sided with Absalom and Ahithophel). At a time when his royal crown was at stake, King David and his men had fled for their lives. Rightly so, they escaped. As he suffered all this, David's wish for wings like a dove to fly away and take refuge in the desert figuratively came true. He did flee to the desert for refuge, even though he didn't get the dove's wings!

David and his men suffered. Wandering in the wilderness, they were hungry, dirty, and tired. He bore the forsaking of family and friends, and the crushing pressures of politics. But he remained under it all, as we shall see. What accounted for his being able to endure?

While David and his men rightly escaped the immediate danger, could he have engineered an overall escape and chosen to end the suffering they were enduring, even though they were on the run? I think it reasonable to say David could have! With the power David wielded and the mastery of war he had gained over the years, he could have easily put to naught his son's schemes, quashed Ahithophel's rebellion, and massacred those who sided with them. David could have made escape and more power his goal, bulldozing these obstacles. But David was different. Why?

David was different because, unlike the Buddha, he knew there was a God to call him to account. This God of the Bible is the same One to whom you and I are accountable today. In his accountability to God in the midst of his suffering, while David escaped immediate danger, he did not see ultimate escape as the solution. He saw all his suffering as coming from the hand of God. He saw Absalom, his son who betrayed him, still dear to his heart. He saw Ahithophel, a dear friend who betrayed him. David saw the future of the nation in the masses who sided with them. What he saw grieved his heart. Yet David didn't seek to escape and establish a utopia. If anything, in a sense that's what Absalom and Ahithophel were doing. Rather, David did what marked him as "a man after God's own heart,"[16] and showed that he knew how to rightly respond to suffering.

David's Solution

David wrote Psalm 55 in the thick of the turmoil we just read about. The first thing that David did, as a suffering man accountable to God, was to pray. His response to suffering began with a prayer for God to hear him. He asked God to answer. Everything else we learn in Psalm 55 about how to respond to suffering is born in prayer—open, earnest, honest, and expectant dialogue with God. Through everything David said to God, he was asking God to intervene and act on his behalf. In telling God why he should intervene, David gives us a pattern for responding to suffering that is more rewarding than escape. I encourage you to have Psalm 55 available to read (Google it if you have to!) as we observe David's pattern.

Baring the Heart and Soul Before God

No one—especially God—expects a suffering person to be pretentious and portray themselves as having it all together when they really don't. Perhaps our social and relational malady of "political correctness" in speech demands that we quash candor when it comes to matters of soul and matters of state. But David was one politician who didn't care for political correctness when he prayed. Here in Psalm 55 (verses 1–8), David let God know exactly what he was experiencing, both personally and as Israel's king.

David let God know that he was moaning in complaint to him because of the pressures he was under. He felt the past grudges that Ahithophel and Absalom harbored against him exploding into present rage. The waves of this explosion reached the very heart of David, so that he shuddered in terror and felt a death-like shroud hanging over him. It was as these feelings churned that he wished to break free and fly away like a dove. David expressed this to God, who David knew understood him intimately. He

---

16. 1 Samuel 13:14 & Acts 13:22

knew God's ear would be attentive to his complaining mouth as he let out the deep frustrations of his heart.

Psychologists use the term "catharsis" to refer to the release of pent-up mental and emotional stress. Catharsis is the Greek word for "purge" or "purify."[17] Psychologists suggest catharsis as normative for a healthy life, through which one can discover the cause of deep-seated emotions, making use of it to "change themselves, their relationships, and their lives."[18] It was Sigmund Freud who made the previously arts-related concept of catharsis a core concept of his psychoanalytic therapy. He tried to bring a client's repressed emotions to the surface by simply letting them retell, and therefore also re-experience, the event that might have led to how they felt. (Of course, most of Freud's catharsis centered mainly on a person's sexual drive and how it affected their current state. I don't think King David would have appreciated Freud's advice if he were Freud's client during this traumatic episode!)

The point that psychologists try to make when suggesting catharsis can simply be boiled down to this: talking to someone helps. And if talking to a severely-limited (and sometimes even profoundly wrong) psychologist can help, what about when one talks to God, the Creator, who is not only willing to listen but able to change the situation? What about when you talk to other people who also know God, and can listen to you and relate? The change that a psychologist's advice can bring goes only as far as the psychologist can perceive. The transformation that the all-knowing God brings to one dependent on him lasts beyond what we can understand or imagine.

The transformation God brings to a person who bares heart and soul to him does not have to do merely with sharing our frustrations, struggles, and anxieties with him. It is *not* merely some sort of spiritual catharsis so we *feel good*. While feeling good may be a by-product, before we can legitimately reap this benefit, there must first be a cleansing of conscience so that we are *good in God's sight*. Before we can bare *the struggles of the soul* to God, a person must first bare *the sin of the soul* to God. In other words, there must first be a confession of sin to God, and a cleansing from sin, before there can ever be healing in suffering. True catharsis of the soul happens only when you turn away from sin, confess it—that is, acknowledge that you have sinned—before God, and receive the healing that is available

---

17. Merriam-Webster's, "Catharsis."
18. Diamond, "Anger and Catharsis: Myth, Metaphor or Reality?"

through Christ's work on the cross, where he paid for sin and all of its effects—including suffering.[19]

While we may think that the verbalizing of emotions for relief and change is something closer to Freud and to our time, David was practicing this all the time. All of his Psalms are soaked with the pouring out of his heart to God—in confessional catharsis, in complete honesty—as he encountered various kinds of suffering over his lifetime. In fact, David is doing here what his son, Absalom, and his friend, Ahithophel, should have done in the first place! They should have bared their hearts and souls to God about David and asked God to intervene. Had they done that early on and not let their anger toward David fester, they would not have found themselves trying to murder him.

When God intervenes on our behalf as we bare our hearts and souls before him, it breaks the circular path of sin, suffering, and attempted self-liberation we are caught in. More importantly, baring our hearts to God shows our utter dependence on him, which draws us into a deeper relationship with him and causes him to receive glory.

Pleading for Justice from God

What secular psychologists today may not understand is that the need for any kind of catharsis ultimately stems from a person's longing for justice—a justice that will change the situation. A lot of suffering is because of injustice. Somewhere, at some time, someone did something that was not right. That person may or may not have been you. Whether or not it was you, because something wrong was done, you now bear the consequences of that wrongful action, and even perpetuate the wrong when you try taking justice into your own hands. You suffer. Whether it's *just suffering* or *unjust suffering*, you suffer anyway, and as long as you suffer, you look for the righting of something that you know is not right. In so doing, you are ultimately pleading for justice. You are seeking resolution.

But to whom does one go when making this plea for justice and seeking resolution? David went to God. He knew that God not only heard him as he poured out his heart and soul before him, but that God was the arbiter and executor of perfect justice in an unjust world.

Here in Psalm 55 (verses 9–15), David asked God to confound the plans of his enemies and bring division among them as they staged their

---

19. Isaiah 53:5

coup and planned their bloody pursuit. The injustice lay in these traitors bringing confusion among the people of the kingdom and dividing their loyalties—so justice demanded that their own plans be confused and that they as usurpers also be divided. David had no qualms in asking for this. He could not bear the fact that those whom he trusted and loved so much had turned on him, like loving lambs morphing into bloodthirsty wolves. He made particular reference to Ahithophel, whom he called his "familiar friend." It is always heart-wrenching to believe for the longest time that someone is your friend, only to realize one day that they never were. Not to forget the even greater pain of having a son turn on you, about which David seemed comparatively silent in Psalm 55.

Being betrayed in cold hatred by a friend or family member is one of the greatest injustices you and I could ever be dealt or could ever deal. Has either of these betrayals been your experience?

David's heart cried out for justice, and he asked God to make death meet his enemies who had masqueraded as his friends. He asked that death come upon them in a deceitful manner. Just as they had been deceitful and had conned David and the rest of the kingdom, let them be conned to their deaths, David reasoned before God. "After all," said David (I am paraphrasing), "very evil lives among them. So it would be better for You, O God, to kill them—for my sake and the sake of the people whose lives they are destroying." What candor! Shocking to our cultured ears maybe, but refreshing to one who is in the heat of this kind of suffering.

When you bare your heart and soul to someone, it is not merely to get emotional relief, but because somewhere deep in your heart, you desire for the very situation to be resolved. When a person knows that perfect justice—flawless and transforming justice—has been administered, it brings relief and peace like nothing else. The catharsis of venting to another (human) person cannot do this. Mere catharsis for the sake of catharsis between human beings, with no change in the situation, is simply another form of escapism which is bound to bring a person full circle after the cathartic effects have worn off. The exception, however, is when we vent to God. God is the only person we can place our confidence in to experience the catharsis which not only relieves but eventually changes situations, by having God transform us and those involved.

Endurance Experts

Placing Confidence in God

When you cry out for justice, the person or system you place confidence in reveals a lot about the kind of person you are. If you place your confidence in yourself, it shows you unwittingly think you are perfectly just. If you and I were perfectly just, we would not be in a situation in which we were crying for justice, would we? If you place your confidence in another person or system for justice, maybe that's a little better than placing confidence in yourself. But since they are human just like you and I, they also aren't perfect enough to bring justice to the situation. Injustice can be righted only by someone who is himself perfectly just and has the power to administer justice. Here in Psalm 55 (verses 16–21), David spoke of his confidence in God.

David reiterated that he would continue to call out to God in the midst of this suffering. Having poured out his heart and soul to God in the face of death and betrayal, the confidence he placed in God was amazingly unshakeable. God, declared David, would surely save him from the opposition he was up against. Whether David cried out to God in the morning, at noon, or in the evening, he was very sure God would hear him and intervene to change the situation in David's favor. Though a battle raged around David for his life and for the throne of his kingdom, God would grant David peace. David's enemies, on the other hand, would be afflicted by God, because they had no fear of God.

You may wonder what King David's main reason was for putting his confidence in God. David expressed in verse 19 that he knew his God was the King who lived and sat on the throne of the universe from before time began. He was the One who was outside time, above time, and in control of all the happenings in the world, including's David's present suffering. As the One above all unjust situations, he is able to administer justice. God is sovereign over the circumstances of the world. God is both just (that is, righteous) *and* the justifier of those who place their confidence in the worthy Savior, Jesus Christ.[20]

Jesus Christ, then, is the one who rights the injustices of this life and straightens the circular road of salvation we are caught in.

God knows our situation and is in control. That's why David placed his confidence in God. Who (or what) are you placing your confidence in as you long for justice and resolution in suffering? David bares his heart and

---

20. Romans 3:23–26

soul, pleads for justice, places his confidence in God, and then encourages his audience—present and future readers—to do the same.

Encouraging Future Readers

Suffering in this life is a burden we carry—a burden that at some point becomes too great for us to bear. If we continue carrying the burden too long, it will crush us, and our suffering will have gotten the better of us. David's advice in responding to suffering is a pattern which, when emulated, is more rewarding than escape. In pouring out his heart and soul, pleading for justice, and placing his confidence in God, David cast his burden on the Lord. That was his encouragement in Psalm 55 (verses 22–23) to all future readers, including you and me. David instructed us to do what he knew worked every time in suffering: "Cast your burden on the Lord and he will sustain you." If you and I want to be sustained in suffering, and not be crushed under the weight of its burden, our only resort is to transfer the burden to a Savior who is strong enough to bear it. When we've done that, there are two ways we are freed.

One, we are guaranteed that anyone who is causing us to suffer will be brought to justice by God. David pronounced something over his enemies that ought to make anyone who is oppressive stop and shiver in their tracks: that they would be brought down to a "pit of destruction" and not live out half their days. As they tried to ascend to power, they would descend in destruction. As they tried to cut David's life short, their lives would be cut short.

Two, once we've transferred our burden to God, we are freed to trust him for the outcome. In some way, at some time, he will indeed favor those who are in the right because they have trusted in the worthy Savior to right the injustices of life and save them, both here and into eternity.

When we are suffering, it brings such relief and freedom of spirit to know that justice will be enforced, and that we can trust our Savior with all of it. Who have you cast your burden on, dear reader? Through praying and telling God all that was on his mind, David cast all that he was faced with into the hands of God, the Almighty.

David's Advice:
Timeless and Relevant in the 21st Century

Now if King David came to you today in the thick of your suffering, giving all this advice on how to respond, you might ask him,

> King David, you don't know how heavy my suffering is. How can you stand there and tell me to just bare my heart and soul to God, to plead for justice, and to place my confidence in him? Why should I follow your advice?

As a person living in the 21st century, this would be a good follow-up question to the ancient king's advice. David's response might sound something like this:

> I may be ancient, but my advice directs you to the One who is eternal. The fact that God heard me and intervened, and helped me through my suffering, and delivered me, and administered justice, and changed the situation in my favor, warrants my encouraging you to put your trust in him as well. I must share this with you because you need it today as much as I did then. Times and cultures may have changed, but two things have not yet changed in this world: that sinful human beings still suffer, and that God delivers and saves the suffering and sinful person who trusts him. God has not changed his ways. He is the same. What he did for me, he will do for you, if you take my advice and trust him to deliver you.

While this dialogue is obviously creative fiction, it represents truth about why David would encourage us today to go to God in our suffering. There is proof that God intervened in David's suffering when he responded by enduring instead of totally escaping. How this account ends shows that it is not escaping and seeking a utopia, but enduring and seeking refuge in God through the suffering, that will finally liberate us—even if one must temporarily lodge in the wilderness. To show you how this is, I must finish narrating the account I began from the Bible, from the book of 2 Samuel (chapters 13–19).

The account of David being pursued by Ahithophel and Absalom ends in tragedy. Treacherous Ahithophel hanged himself simply because Absalom did not heed his plan to assassinate David. Ahithophel, who was trying to establish a utopia with Absalom, in the end could not endure so small an ordeal as having his counsel rejected. How would he have endured the rigors of co-ruling that utopia when his fragile-as-crystal egotistic heart could not endure the rejection of his assassination plot? Such escapists are not born to inherit or rule earthly kingdoms, let alone heavenly ones. When he needed to endure, Ahithophel instead escaped, ending his own life in the clutches of suicide, perhaps not living out half his days, as David prayed in Psalm 55. In escaping, he traded his earthly suffering for an eternity of endless suffering.

Absalom, on the other hand, did not take his own life—but it was taken from him. With Ahithophel dead, Absalom's treachery against his father culminated in war between his own army and David's faithful men. Absalom's men came out from Jerusalem, and David's men came out from the wilderness. The place of their convergence was the deadly forest of Ephraim, which turned into their battleground. As Absalom rode his mule in the forest, he came upon David's men. The mule passed under the twisted branches of an oak tree, and Absalom's long hair got tangled in the branches. As the mule rode out from under him, Absalom was left suspended midair. David's men who found Absalom dared not touch the king's son, because of David's command to deal gently with him. However, when they reported to their commander, Joab, that Absalom was suspended by his hair from an oak tree, Joab wasted no time in rushing to the spot and thrusting three spears through Absalom's heart. Then Joab's armor bearers were emboldened to further ravage Absalom to make sure he was dead. Finally, they took Absalom's body, threw it into a pit in the forest, and covered it with a pile of stones. Absalom certainly did not live out half his days, and whether or not David meant it literally in Psalm 55 (verse 23), Absalom was brought down to a pit—dead and destroyed.

David stood vindicated, delivered, and liberated from his present suffering. He had to grieve over the loss of his son Absalom and would suffer more, as we read later in the narrative, but that suffering was perhaps far less compared to the greater suffering he would have gone through, had God allowed the treacherous coup to succeed.

Why should you and I heed the ancient king's advice today? Very simply, because those who heed this advice will not be disappointed but rewarded. The reward, as we saw in David's case, is given by God. God steps into the situation. God saves the suffering person who endures by trusting in him. God rights the injustices of life that cause suffering, and brings justice, peace, and resolution. Not only does God intervene in this life, but his deliverance lasts beyond this life. Deliverance may not come in the form we hope for in this lifetime, but it will most assuredly come when we cross the finish line of the marathon of suffering and step into eternity. In eternity, God will right all the injustices that have not been righted in the here and now. Thus, David's advice is timeless for suffering and endurance, which lasts only for a short time. Again, the pattern David exemplifies for us in suffering is:

- Bare your heart and soul before God.
- Plead with God for justice.
- Place your confidence in God.
- Encourage other suffering people to do the same before, during, and after God intervenes in your situation.

Through this process, God will cause good to come even in your suffering. That's why you and I should heed this advice today. One thing I am convinced of, which I ask you to consider and be convinced of yourself, is this: escapism eventually leads to utopianism of some sort. People who escape the reality of suffering, because they do not know how to respond, end up living in a fantasy world. This is true both for individuals and for entire nations. History has proven this again and again. You escape some earthly suffering you cannot endure, and look for something better, something that suits *your ideal* of the heavenly. We just saw the example of David, contrasted with Ahithophel and Absalom. David endured suffering and was liberated, temporal and eternal joy following him. Ahithophel and Absalom looked to escape all suffering and build their utopia, but died, eternal sorrow following them.

Closer to our own time, what happens when a man continually escapes suffering, becomes delusional, and then turns into a raving mad utopian?

Chapter 3

Coming Full Circle: East or West, this World is not Heaven

IF WE ARE REALISTIC, we will concede that while heaven is real, this present world is clearly not heaven. Let me say it again. Heaven is real, but this present world is not heaven. If we attempt to create heaven on earth, we may actually end up creating a hell of sorts, sowing the seeds for the future suffering of ourselves and others. History has proven it time and again.

I would rather not use the example of Adolf Hitler here. But he is such great proof that the Escapist Utopianism of Ahithophel and Absalom is alive closer to our times, that I cannot resist displaying him in the hall of shame to warn people to stay clear of this path. If ever there was one, Hitler was an escapist who turned into an "escapist utopian." Allow me to explain.

A Mad Man is Raised

Adolf Hitler was brought up by parents who were polar opposites in the way they treated him—his mother giving into to his every fancy and his father forcing obedience with harshness. Historian Alan Bullock sheds light on Adolf's upbringing. Born in 1889,

> Adolf left the Linz Realschule in 1904 not because his mother was too poor to pay the fees, but because his record at school was so indifferent that he had to accept a transfer to another school at Steyr, where he finished his education at sixteen. . . . There is no doubt that he did not get along well with his father . . . his father

was dissatisfied with his school reports and made his dissatisfaction plain.[21]

But Adolf was unperturbed by his father's dissatisfaction. His younger days were marked by a failure in stability and discipline, because of foolishness on both his part and his parents'. These were followed by the failure to learn from the failures, and then the failure to endure failure so as to use it as a stepping stone to true success. Adolf threw caution to the wind and moved forward with reckless abandon, pursuing his unrealistic and utopian ideals. The seeds of suffering—his own and others'—were being sown. Bullock continues,

> Hitler glossed over his poor performance at school, which he left in 1905 without securing the customary Leaving Certificate. *He found every possible excuse for himself*, from illness and his father's tyranny to artistic ambition and political prejudice. *It was a failure which rankled and found frequent expression* in sneers at the 'educated gentlemen' with their diplomas and doctorates.[22] (Emphasis mine)

It is quite like an escapist to find excuses not to endure the hard work needed to succeed, isn't it? It is also quite like an escapist to fail and never learn because they regress down the dreamy path of utopianism, which is so disconnected from reality that it can import nothing from the dream world into the real world. Bullock continues that Hitler

> ... refused to earn his living and spent the next two years indulging in dreams of becoming an artist or an architect, living at home, filling his sketch book with entirely unoriginal drawings and elaborating grandiose plans of rebuilding Linz.... He lived in a world of his own, content to let his mother provide for his needs, *scornfully refusing to concern himself with such petty and mundane affairs as money or a job.*[23] (Emphasis mine)

Escapist utopians want nothing to do with the harsh realities of everyday existence, because it is a sort of suffering for them. They would rather skip to making their grandiose ideas a reality. The Bible, in the book of Proverbs (25:14), likens such people to clouds and winds without rain. Again, Bullock says of Hitler,

21. Bullock, *Hitler*, 4–11.
22. Bullock, *Hitler*, 4–11.
23. Bullock, *Hitler*, 4–11.

Coming Full Circle

> His ambition was now to enter the Academy of Fine Arts in Vienna. His first attempt to enter the Academy in October 1907 was unsuccessful.... The director advised him to try his talents in the direction of architecture: he was not cut out to be a painter. *But Hitler refused to admit defeat.* In mid-September [1908] Hitler had again applied for admission to the Academy of Art. This time, he was not even admitted to the examination.[24] (Emphasis mine)

There is a line that divides faith, which perseveres in the real world, from folly, which refuses to ever be corrected when told it is pursuing a fantasy. In this context, folly proves to be folly because it is closed to advice about reality. Eventually a person could harm him- or herself, and many others, in the wake of unrepentant folly. Bullock writes,

> [Towards 1911] He started a score of jobs but failed to make anything of them and relapsed in to the old hand-to-mouth existence, living by expedience and little spurts of activity. As time passed, these habits became ingrained, and he became more eccentric, more turned in on himself.[25]

When a person repeatedly pursues what he is powerless to perform apart from God—"apart from God" being the operative phrase—and fails to admit defeat, he works himself into a frenzy in order to succeed and prove his point. He then becomes disconnected from reality, and begins escaping to a reality of his own making—in other words, a world of fantasy, a utopia—which he seeks to impose on other people by force. Hitler's personal escapism eventually led to a personal utopianism. And because no one was prudent or bold enough to stop him at the personal level, what was his own weakness became the weakness of the poor German masses, and they came under the sway of Hitler's Escapist Utopianism at the national level. The seeds of suffering that were sown in the heart of Hitler, un-nipped in the bud, came to full bloom in the soil of those German minds that supported him.

History records Hitler's rise to power as he revived a collapsed economy in five years, erased Germany's shame from World War I by reclaiming the Rhineland, and with many more accomplishments gave Germans a reason to believe they would become great again.[26] Before long, with his broken-cross swastika, Hitler sought to inaugurate a utopia he believed was

---

24. Bullock, *Hitler*, 4–11.
25. Bullock, *Hitler*, 4–11.
26. Lutzer, *Hitler's Cross*, 17.

the Third Reich—essentially a marriage of Church and State—assuming the historic mantle of Charlemagne's First Reich and Otto von Bismarck's Second Reich.[27]

A Utopia is Sought

Read a few of Hitler's words, from his fiery speeches made to the German public.

> The German people are no longer a people of shame and degradation. *No more weakness and lack of faith* for the German people, no! *Lord, they are strong* once more, in mind, in will, in determination and *endurance*.[28] (Emphasis mine)

The seeds of suffering—the suffering of Jews and Germans alike—were now bearing fruit.

Ah, here is a deranged lunatic who thinks he has become an endurance expert, of all things! Do you see that in his speech? He has been deluded into thinking that he has faith, strength, and endurance when in reality it is just the opposite: doubt, weakness, and escapism. He has everyone under the same delusion. It is quite like an escapist utopian not only to *fail*, but to *try to succeed* in the face of obviously impending failure, at everybody else's expense. As an escapist utopian, Hitler—through his fiery oratory and diabolical media-driven propaganda—made the masses believe the lie that he was building them up, when in reality he was taking them all down with him to the abyss. So he shouted,

> All this is your doing. Without you Germany could never have been saved. Your courage and perseverance have earned you the right to consider yourselves *the saviours of your people*.[29] (Emphasis mine)

It is quite like escapist utopians to seek saviors from among men. It is also quite like escapist utopians to present themselves as the saviors of men, and make men believe it. Leaders who are escapist utopians induce a self-savior mentality in their followers. But most importantly, please allow me to say at this point, it is quite like escapist utopians "not to turn"—and

---

27. Lutzer, *Hitler's Cross*, 20–24.
28. TheKbeal, "Hitler's Utopia-Power."
29. TheKbeal, "Hitler's Utopia-Power."

simultaneously bar others from turning—to the one Savior of all men, Jesus Christ.

Escapist utopians seek utopias; and when they cannot find one, they try desperately to create one. But the creation of a false heaven on earth involves the destruction of everything and everyone that does not fit the designer's blueprint. When humans take on the prerogative of creating heaven in this world, instead of waiting for God's Heaven, they end up creating a sort of hell on earth—having to annihilate all things and people that obstruct their agenda. This is exactly what Hitler did. Renowned Holocaust scholar and German historian Peter Longerich hits the nail on the head when he says,

> But this goal remained an *unrealisable utopian ideal*, not least because the 'races' existed only in *the fantasy world of the Nazis*. The racial homogeneity they desired could only be created negatively, through discrimination, exclusion and eradication—and ultimately by killing those who did not fit into their perfect 'Aryan' society.[30] (Emphasis mine)

In the end, Hitler escaped once and for all, ending his own life in the clutches of suicide just a day after he married. Pathetic indeed. This man who believed he had faith, strength, and endurance, who sought to annihilate everyone who stood against him, took the easy route of escape when faced with the collapse of his utopian fantasy. I think it's clear that we should never follow the path of such escapist utopians as Hitler, or others who espouse similar ideals. Today these philosophies are promoted under the guise of more peaceful and all-inclusive banners, such as liberalism that tolerates anything except the truth.

Why is it so important that we continue to be on our guard against these philosophies today? Let's imagine Hitler answered this question just before he committed suicide. Let's imagine he had some remorse and sobered up a little bit to talk some sense before he took his life (which is very unlikely, but this dialogue is creative fiction anyway). His answer may have been something along these lines, so as to dissuade the questioner who wants to dabble in Escapist Utopianism:

> Beware! You should never heed my utopian philosophy because it will always disappoint, and never reward you. I have discovered this all too late: my ideas come from a world of fantasy I inhabited, and they can never be made compatible with the real world. I sold

30. Longerich, "The Nazi Racial State."

this fantasy to the German masses, and I made it seem attractive for a short time. But I have damned people either for their lives, or for their lives and beyond. And I wonder . . . What lies beyond for them, and for me?

But you be concerned about your lives, and don't fall prey to this folly again. It is a way of life that does not sync with reality, and that has been proven time and again—from Ahithophel and Absalom, to me, Adolf Hitler. Why then would *you* follow it?

However, the sad reality is that people in the global West, in this very generation I belong to, are turning to Escapist Utopianism—whether they are aware of it or not—in highly innocuous forms that purport to be peaceful and loving. How do I know this? Well, there was more to Hitler's Escapist Utopianism than meets the human eye. Something was going on in the spiritual realm with him, and the same is happening today.

Two Eastern Influences on the Battleground of Western Minds: Expectant Endurance versus Escapist Utopianism

By the West, I specifically mean the United States and Europe today, but also the Western and westernized cultures of the world at large. In his delusion, Hitler thought of himself as the epitome of the Western man as he propagated his "unrealizable utopian ideal" of a perfect Aryan society. What many do not know, however, is that Hitler was influenced by Eastern mystical and occult forces. Between his first failed attempt to enter the Academy of Fine Arts in Vienna in 1907, and his second failed attempt in 1911, while in Vienna he

> . . . spent all his free time in the Hofberg Library, reading books on history and the occult. He became an expert in Eastern religions and was known to purchase such books in used book stores, and then resell them so he could buy more. [31]

Hitler became fascinated with a spear in the Hofberg library that was rumored to be the spear that pierced the side of Jesus Christ on the cross. One day Hitler heard a tour guide say, *"This spear is shrouded in mystery;*

---

31. Lutzer, *Christ Among Other gods,* 163–4.

whoever unlocks its secrets will rule the world."[32] Hitler believed the lie and it gripped him. Further, Hitler believed that the Emperor Constantine had possessed the spear, and that forty-five Roman emperors had also held it while ruling. A young Hitler, bewitched by the spear and the thought of ruling the world, thus opened himself up to demonic activity. Later on, when Hitler rose to power, he surrounded himself with people who were committed occultists. In fact, the original members of the Nazi party were hardcore Satanists who brought Hitler to deeper levels of "spiritual perception."[33] When Hitler conquered Vienna, he took the spear for himself from the Hofberg Library, embracing it as if the world itself was being handed to him.

Hitler, who believed in the superiority of the Aryan race—the concept of "Aryan" originally coming from Eastern, Hindu scriptures—was a Western man thoroughly influenced by Eastern spiritual forces of, please note, the diabolical and destructive sort.

Now both the Escapist Utopianism that I have written about thus far, and the Expectant Endurance which I will write about, are originally—historically and geographically speaking—Eastern worldviews. They had their origin in the Eastern hemisphere, and from that origin have flowed to and impacted the West.

Escapist Utopianism from the East, in the West

As I illustrated in Chapter 1, Escapist Utopianism comes from religions like Buddhism (though those religions obviously do not call themselves escapist utopians). Hinduism also teaches a similar path, with its mantras and tantras which are supposed to help people escape the clutches of karma. In the end, their *chakra* ("circle" or "wheel" in Hindi) ends up making a *bakra* ("goat" in Hindi) of people! Neither of these religions believe in a heaven after this earthly life; instead they believe that the human soul ultimately merges with some supreme force, or continues in a cycle of reincarnation. For them there is no such place such as heaven, because there is no belief in an eternal, living, and loving person who has gone to prepare such a place for them. As Richard Philips wrote, expressing the Buddha's view of God, "There is no God to call thee to account."[34]

32. Lutzer, *Christ Among Other gods*, 163–4.
33. Lutzer, *Christ Among Other gods*, 163–4.
34. Phillips, *The Story of Gautama Buddha*, 128.

Since there is no God to call people to account, there can also be no God to "call" people to heaven, can there? Think about it. And if there is no God *and* no heaven, in the inescapable and inevitable suffering that people go through, they are bound to create gods for themselves here on earth to try to alleviate their suffering. But God and the place of His dwelling, Heaven, have always been and forever will be associated one with another. So while escapist utopians take up the task of creating gods, they simultaneously create make-believe heavens on earth to accompany those gods, for by a universal law of association there must be a heaven where there are gods. Except that these religions and their here-and-now versions of heaven are essentially earthly lifestyles which erroneously suppose that a person has achieved what is only achievable in God's real Heaven.

For example, Buddhism teaches people to kill desire to achieve complete enlightenment. Hinduism teaches people to do certain good deeds and perform rituals which will break the karmic cycle and liberate the entrapped soul. Hedonism, which is an irreligion made popular by the Greeks and is the opposite of Buddhism's killing of desire, teaches people to live out their unbridled lusts to achieve complete satisfaction. At least that's what they think will happen. But the Bible teaches that while we have previews of these on earth, all three of these goals—total enlightenment, total liberation, and complete satisfaction—can and will be achieved only when we get to God's real Heaven. To think that total enlightenment, total liberation, and complete satisfaction can be fully achieved in the here and now is an illusion, an escaping of the reality of suffering in pursuit of "a better reality," which turns out in the end to be a fantasy.

That's a description of Escapist Utopianism, and as we've already seen, it comes from the East. But it clearly holds sway in the West today. What else can you conclude when you walk into a Hindu temple in metropolitan USA and see a predominantly Western, Caucasian group of people worshipping gods of Eastern Hindu mythology, or practicing Yoga with its chants of "Om?" I've seen all this with my own eyes. Or when you meet an African-American Hindu priest, who thinks that in his past life he was certainly a great Hindu priest from Nepal or India? I've met such a person, in a Chicago Hindu Temple. Are Westerners not turning to Eastern mystical religions because of the lure of the so-called liberation these worldviews offer them, minus the wrongly perceived "restrictions" that the God of Judeo-Christian Scriptures "imposes" on their happiness and fun? And isn't this proof that the West, whether there is awareness or not, has been infiltrated by Eastern philosophies of escapism and has turned to seek the utopias promised by them? If you want more proof, just look at the number of Hindu or Buddhist Temples, or even the Mosques that have dotted the American landscape in the last fifty or so years. More than that, see the number of Westerners who attend these houses of worship. One doesn't even need to see hard numbers and statistics to realize that much of the West is under the sway of Eastern escapist philosophies.

The late 1800s were times of both industrialization and greater ethnic influx for the United States. The influx of various ethnicities brought with them their religious viewpoints. America was also gradually turning away from its Puritan, Judeo-Christian foundations of the past. This was especially true in the universities where the German higher criticism had done its damage, undermining Christianity and causing people to doubt the veracity and authenticity of the Bible. It was the perfect time for America to welcome these Eastern escapist worldviews. And so these worldviews have been making inroads into America since Swamy Vivekananda came to the Parliament of World Religions in Chicago in 1893. From then till today, untold numbers of Americans have dabbled in Eastern mystical and occult religions in a bid to escape suffering, and have rejected the God of the Bible, whose laws and love have shaped this nation. Only turning back to the true God will help people make any sense of suffering in life.

Expectant Endurance from the East, also in the West

The principle and practice of "Expectant Endurance" (as I would like to call it) come from the Judeo-Christian Scriptures, whose authors—such as David in Psalm 55—were inspired by God, and who through their experience encouraged people to endure the various sufferings of this life, with the expectation of being rewarded by God. Why did these biblical men and women endure and encourage others to endure suffering? The great reason for their enduring of suffering was because they believed in, and looked forward to, the reality of Heaven. For them back then, and for us today who believe the same,

> . . . this momentary, light affliction is producing for us an eternal weight of glory far beyond all comparison, while we look not at the things which are seen, but at the things which are not seen; for the things which are seen are

temporal, but the things which are not seen are eternal.
(1 Corinthians 4:17–18)

Though the real Heaven talked about here is not seen in the now, this real Heaven exists—unlike the heavens escapist utopians dream up. It will be well worth it to endure all the sufferings of this life, because we will see that real Heaven one day. When we get to the real Heaven and look back, our present sufferings will have felt like a feather compared to the weight of the reality of being with God in Heaven then. The weight of God's glory in Heaven, which we will witness and share in, will eclipse and erase all earthly suffering.

This introduces us to the Judeo-Christian practice of Expectant Endurance, and like Escapist Utopianism, it comes from the East. But also like Escapist Utopianism, it holds sway in the West today. For what else can you conclude when you walk into a metropolitan American church which believes the biblical and historical tenets of Christianity—the reality of God, the reality of Heaven, and the Savior who grants access to both—and see Westerners and Easterners together holding to the faith of their fathers, in spite of the culture selling out to Escapist Utopianism? What else can you conclude but that they are practicing endurance with the expectation of being rewarded? I see this with my eyes, and though I am from the East myself, having now lived in the West for more than one third of my life, I also participate in this Expectant Endurance with all my being. I participate in this with hundreds of others who attend the church where I am on staff, The Moody Church in Chicago. We have people from over 70 nations of the world represented at The Moody Church; people from both East and West who live life through the worldview of Expectant Endurance. There are countless other people the world over, all part of the Church of Jesus Christ, who hold to this same worldview of Expectant Endurance.

People in the West who endure suffering have stuck to this Judeo-Christian biblical worldview of Expectant Endurance—because the God we worship, who has proven the reliability of His character and His promises over and over again, has promised eternal life and freedom from all suffering. This is also proof that, in a Western world being overrun by Eastern Escapist Utopianism, there still remains a people willing to expectantly endure earthly suffering because of the reality of Heaven. A remnant in the West still holds to Expectant Endurance, an Eastern philosophy that historically goes back to before King David's time, and points ultimately to the Lord Jesus Christ Himself.

Coming Full Circle

What we have then today are two Eastern influences —Escapist Utopianism and Expectant Endurance—which both exist on Western soil, though at odds with each other. Thus Western minds have become the battleground for two Eastern beliefs. The questions are these: on the battleground of your mind, which Eastern belief is winning the battle? And what evidence do you need to know which one is winning?

Chapter 4

The Response to Suffering: The Gigantic Secret of the Christian

Sir Isaac Newton set forth his theories of gravitation in 1666, when he was only 23. In 1686, Newton then postulated the now well-known three laws of motion, which were printed in a work called the *Principia Mathematica Philosophiae Naturali*. If you are thankful for air travel today, it may interest you to know that it was Newton's laws of motion that were instrumental in helping the Wright brothers invent, build, and successfully fly the first air machine—the Wright Flyer—in 1903. Germane to our discussion is Newton's third law of motion, which states,

> To every action there is always opposed an equal reaction.[35]

Or, as the more familiar version reads, "To every action there is an equal and opposite reaction." Newton was right to use the word "reaction" and not "response." In the world of physics, the word "reaction" connotes an object being bound by an unalterable law, to which it can only react. For every action or force imposed upon an inanimate and non-sentient object, the object must, and can only, react to that force in a manner consistent with the laws of nature, which Newton so brilliantly discovered and described. So in the world of inanimate, non-sentient objects, "reaction" is the right word. However, in the world of sentient and animate beings, "reaction" is a poor word. "Response" is a better word. Just as "reaction" connotes *something* being *bound* by an unalterable law, "response" connotes

---

35. Newton, *Mathematical Principles of Natural Philosophy*, 83.

someone being able to *rise above* universal laws to alter them under specific conditions.

In life, you and I often find ourselves "reacting" to situations, don't we? For instance, by default we exude negativity in suffering. Sometimes it seems as if we, although sentient beings, are powerless to respond—and have no choice but to react—when acted upon by external forces in life. The truth, however, is that we do have the choice and the ability to rise above the laws of nature, to respond to circumstances rather than reacting. We are not, or at least do not have to be, governed by Newton's third law in responding to life's circumstances, including suffering. "How is that the case?" you ask. "How do we rise above laws that seem indelibly written into the nature of the cosmos, and into human nature?"

Rising Above, to Respond

You and I cannot alter the physical law of action/reaction which Newton discovered. But when it comes to applying it to life—when applying this physical law of nature metaphysically (to our existence and identity)—there is a way to bypass its rule. And that way is by rising above, to the One who is above—to God.

The laws of nature are not laws unto themselves. They were ordained and set by God, the Creator and Designer of the universe. Nature's laws are, in fact, God's laws. Therefore he can rule and overrule the laws of nature and yet remain consistent with his own character. Just as he is above the physical cosmos and the working of nature, so too God is above our carnal, human makeup, and he gives us the ability to respond to suffering instead of reacting. In other words, God frees us from the universal law that by default binds us to react negatively in suffering, enabling us rather to respond in a manner that pleases him, and benefits us.

Only the Christian, biblical worldview affords human beings the opportunity to be freed from the Salvation in Circles mentality (Chapter 1), and from the universal law of being stuck in reaction mode as we suffer. Other religions may offer options. But God alone, in Jesus Christ, frees us to rise above circumstances and respond rightly. Responding rightly involves a change in perspective, a switch from an earthly point of view to a heavenly one, because of which we see things as God sees them and are able to respond rightly to our suffering. For the Christian who suffers, Newton's third law when applied metaphysically can read, "To every action there *does not have to be* an equal and opposite reaction. *There can be* an unequal and opportune response instead."

The Right Response to Suffering

I ended Chapter 3 by asking what evidence is needed to prove whether Escapist Utopianism or Expectant Endurance is winning on the battleground of your mind. That is, what evidence do you need to prove you are responding rightly, and expectantly enduring your own suffering? Now for the answer.

If you and I are rightly responding to suffering and expectantly enduring, we will have the presence of one element in life that overrides and undergirds our suffering: we will have joy.[36] If an overriding and undergirding joy is absent through suffering—if we can't ever rejoice through suffering, if we can't ever see the light at the end of the tunnel of this life, if we never have hope in suffering, if we never have spiritual rest—it means we are not responding rightly. We are reacting. Suffering is getting the better of us, instead of us being bettered by God through suffering.

On the other hand, if joy is present through suffering—if we can rejoice even when down, if we can see the light at the end of the tunnel of this life, if we can hope through seeming hopelessness, if we do have spiritual rest—it means we are responding as God would have us. It's a little three letter word in English—J-O-Y—which is an immense encouragement as we run the marathon of life toward the finish line. Joy. We sing about it during the Christmas season, but ought to live it out perennially. In the opening lines of James' letter to first-century Christians, the Bible says,

> Consider it all joy, my brethren, when you encounter various trials. (James 1:2)

The right response to the sufferings of life should be joy. Before we consider this *response* of joy in depth, let us better set the context. First notice the *recipients* of James' letter; then notice three *realities* in connection with suffering.

---

36. It is not my intention to have a long discussion about the differences between "joy" and "happiness" in this work. Many people hold that there is a clear distinction between the two, and many works exist to explain this. For the sake of the argument in the context of this book, I hold to the distinction that happiness is available to all human beings, whereas "true joy" in suffering, as I explain it here, is the exclusive privilege of one who is in a personal relationship with Jesus Christ.

THE RESPONSE TO SUFFERING

The Recipients: Real People

James, the half-brother of Jesus Christ, was writing to his "brethren," his Christian brothers and sisters who were suffering a great deal in the first century A.D. These Christians were being persecuted, often to the death, by both Roman officials and Jewish religious leaders. Their suffering was unlike anything you and I will probably ever face in our lifetimes. Yet it is these very people who had the privilege of responding with joy through suffering. Why is responding with joy through suffering the exclusive privilege of Christians? In the next two paragraphs, allow me to repeat what I wrote in the Introduction, and pick it up thereafter.

In the marathon race of life, the Christian can be likened to a marathon runner who successfully endures the rigors of training for and running a marathon. But to receive the medal from God for endurance, one must know God through his Son Jesus Christ. This is the first step, just as one must first register with the organizers of the Chicago Marathon to participate. Not just anyone can jump in at any time to the Chicago Marathon! Try, and authorities may pull you from the race! Besides all the training before the race, you must have your name registered with the organizers, be given a marathon bib with your number on it, and then run to receive a medal at the end of the race. Similarly, only when your name is registered with God, written in Heaven in the book of life—only when you have believed on God's Son Jesus Christ and received the new life he imparts—does he supply all you need to endure the suffering in your life. We must first come to Christ, who himself endured suffering with joy; we must learn from him, and then will be on our way to becoming endurance experts.

Perhaps you have not yet come to Christ, and you are contemplating your own suffering as you read this. Perhaps this is the time the voice of Christ calls to you. When you receive him as your Savior, he will forgive your sins. He will also give you meaning in your suffering, in the light of what he himself endured.

Yes, the Lord Jesus endured suffering, the worst suffering that a human being shall ever have to endure. He endured the suffering of dying on a cross to pay for the sins of those who would believe upon him. But he endured because of the joy that lay ahead of him on the other side of his suffering. In the endurance race of life, the Bible says we are to fix "our eyes on Jesus, the author and perfecter of our faith, who for the joy set before him endured the cross, despising the shame, and has sat down at the right hand of the throne of God" (Hebrews 12:2). Or, as another version reads, "Because of the joy awaiting him, he endured the cross, disregarding its shame" (NLT).

Jesus endured suffering because of the *prospect* of joy, which led to the *presence* of joy in suffering. More on this verse from Hebrews, and on the example of the Lord Jesus Christ through suffering, in Chapter 5. For now, would it not be fair to say that since Jesus' anchor through his suffering was joy, only those who believe in him and follow him can respond with joy in the midst of suffering? That's why James addresses this to Christians. But there are other reasons he does so.

Three Realities: Real Suffering, Real Escapism, Real Joy

Real Suffering

Christians are to respond with joy, James says, "when you encounter various trials . . . " Notice the word "when." In the Christian, biblical worldview, suffering is a given. It is not a question of "if" I suffer as a Christian, but "when." The Christian, biblical worldview recognizes the reality of suffering in life. But there are some worldviews that say everything is an illusion, thereby denying the reality of suffering.

Real Escapism

Some branches of Hinduism, for example, say that everything in the universe is *maya* or illusion.[37] The only way one can transcend this illusory state, they say, is by "cultivating the quality of goodness" by which "the soul may rise to transcendence and escape the clutches of *maya*."[38] First, it's no surprise that escapism is advocated here. Second, how can one escape something when everything is, or everything is perceived to be, illusory? If one cultivates the quality of goodness, won't that too be illusory? Further, if the escape is made, how does the escapee know whether they have really escaped or not, or if their escape is also an illusion? This is rather sad advice for one who is suffering.

---

37. Jayaram, "The Definition and Concept of Maya in Hinduism."
38. The Heart of Hinduism, "Maya: Illusion."

The Response to Suffering

Now before I write anything else, lest you misconstrue that I'm saying Christianity demands some sort of masochism, or a love for suffering—please understand that the Christian, biblical worldview is *all for* helping people through suffering, for easing the burdens of those who suffer, so that their suffering ends. Whether that help manifests through physical means such as therapy, exercise, or medical healing, or through spiritual means such as soul care and counseling, we wish to see people thrive. There is ample proof throughout history that the compassion of Christ has compelled Christians the world over to care for suffering people: for the sick, dying, or troubled in soul and mind. The same is the case today.

We are called to help those who suffer. However, we must be cautious about the origins and intentions of the means we use to do so—because those intentions and origins of the means often determine the outcome. What if the means we use lead to greater suffering in the long run, even if it provides temporary relief?

With that clarification, there is another branch of Hinduism that accepts the reality of suffering (to an extent) but proposes that the solution lies in the practice of Yoga. "Yoga," they say, "promises to free us from suffering."[39] Quoting Hindu texts, a Yoga practitioner here in the West explains this promise—what I am labelling a form of Escapist Utopianism—saying,

> First and foremost, yoga is for the mind, not the body... Yoga Sutra 1.3 says that as a result of yoga or sustained, focused attention, the Self or Seer... is established... In other words, by focusing and refining the mind through yoga, you gain clearer perception and learn to distinguish the mind, body, and emotions from your true essence or Self.[40]

This ought to clear the misconception that many people hold (genuine, Bible-believing followers of Jesus Christ included) that Yoga is just a form of "stretching." Let's try to dispel Western ignorance about an Eastern practice here. According to the Hindu text quoted above, Yoga is clearly not just "stretching" the body. It is for the mind, and therefore turns out to be a spiritual endeavor that leaves the door open to unnecessary and increased suffering. It may not pose spiritual hindrances immediately and may even give great physical relief. But be warned: eventually, if one continues down the road of Yoga, it *could* leave the door open to spiritual attacks. Continuing from the above quote, observe the emphasis given to "Self" by this yogi:

39. Holocombe, "Reduce Suffering."
40. Holocombe, "Reduce Suffering."

> You come to know that Self and act from that place of the Self, thus reducing your experience of suffering . . . From this place of connection, you can observe your emotions and reactions and recognize them as separate from your true nature, valid and painful though they may be. This is the promise of yoga.[41]

You are supposed to dissect your "self" into the constituent facets of mind, emotion, and spirit, which are distinct from your "self," and this is "a place of connection?" Really? If you have just broken down the parts of the "self," how is there connectedness? Or with what or who are you connecting?

You say, "I don't really think about all this when practicing Yoga." Well, you should. I believe there is a connection made indeed, if one follows the Yoga road down to its intended destination. The etymology of the word Yoga has to do with a Sanskrit word which literally means "yoking"[42] or "union." The goal is union with spiritual forces.

Now, this *does not* mean anyone who has ever struck a yoga pose or done yoga as a form of exercise is doomed to be united with spiritual darkness. No. But neither should people be ignorant about the spiritual origins of Yoga. Intention matters here! If one throws caution to the wind, thinking you are immune from even *potential spiritual attacks* when practicing a form of pagan worship, then over time, union with spiritual darkness could become a reality. The same is true of Transcendental Meditation or other forms of Eastern (or Western) mystical, occultic practices. The strategy of the Enemy of the soul, the Devil, is indeed to break down the "self" before entering, just as the strategy of an enemy in war is to divide and conquer.

When this yogi says Yoga is for "reducing your experience of suffering . . . This is the promise of yoga," do you notice there is something that is conspicuously missing in the long run? Yoga *promises* to "reduce" suffering (and I suggest you take that promise with a huge grain of salt!). But for the sake of argument, even if Yoga can follow through on its promise to reduce suffering, it cannot and does not promise joy in the midst of suffering. The promise of joy is conspicuously absent in the yogic worldview. Yogis are still left hankering after something else to give them joy. Absent joy in suffering, Yoga proves to be yet another form of escapism. (In fact, any framework other than the one that offers joy in suffering is escapism.) One has to choose between the passing "promise of yoga" or the enduring promise of

---

41. Holocombe, "Reduce Suffering."
42. Merriam-Webster's, "Yoga."

joy Christ offers in suffering, for the two worldviews are ultimately at odds with each other.

Real Joy: The Response

Only in the Christian, biblical worldview is the reality of suffering recognized, while at the same time the reality of joy offered to us. James wrote to Christians who recognized the harsh reality of suffering in the first century A.D. What was their response to be?

> *Consider it all joy, my brethren*, when you encounter various trials. (James 1:2)

"Considering" or counting suffering as joy was to be their response, and it is to be ours today. But what an odd response to ask of people who are suffering. There is someone who has just lost a loved one, or someone who has just lost a job, or someone who has just found out they have a possibly fatal medical condition, and they are to "consider it all joy"? What does it mean for the Christian to "consider it all joy" when passing through suffering?

Well, it certainly is not a fake-it-till-you-make-it type of pretense that is commanded here. The Christian is not to *act* joyful in suffering, as if nothing were wrong. That would be a form of denial, which is tantamount to escaping suffering. The Christian is to actually *be* joyful in suffering. As I mentioned earlier in this chapter, the *prospect* of joy brings the *presence* of joy. And the Christian has joy not just prospectively, but presently with us on the journey, in the person of the Holy Spirit. The Bible teaches that the Holy Spirit produces joy in us (Galatians 5:22). I cannot emphasize enough that the Holy Spirit produces joy in a Christian through suffering. It is a supernatural, otherwise inexplicable phenomenon we experience in suffering.

We can consider suffering "as a welcome friend,"[43] because through it, God is adding something good to our lives. Having the mindset that God uses suffering as a means to something good on the other end of it, helps us experience the reality of joy in suffering, and helps us endure suffering, coming through it bettered by God. The word "consider," or "count," has to do with accounting and finance. It has to do with how we evaluate suffering. Do we think of suffering as something that is ruining us, or some-

---

43. MacArthur, *James*, 21.

thing by which God is remaking us? For the atheist, agnostic, naturalist, or someone of another worldview with no God, since there is no God behind the sufferings of life, suffering is ruining life and therefore must be escaped. But for the Christian, because God is behind it, every time we suffer we can choose to respond with joy at the prospect of good. If we evaluate suffering as a *good investment* that will yield *great interests* in the future, even though for the present it is painful, we can indeed respond with joy.

All of this, of course, is easier said than done, and is not learned overnight or by osmosis. It has to do rather with a mindset and outlook rooted in the suffering of Christ, that mirrors his mindset and outlook in suffering. As Warren Wiersbe, former Senior Pastor of The Moody Church, said:

> Our values determine our evaluations. If we value comfort more than character, then trials will upset us. If we value the material and physical more than the spiritual, we will not be able to 'count it all joy.' If we live only for the present and forget the future, then trials will make us bitter, not better. [44]

The way to experience real joy in the midst of present suffering has much to do with what is promised in the future, both the immediate and the eternal. When suffering, we tend to forget the future. Blinded by pain and hurt, we don't—and sometimes can't—see hope. We become hopeless. But the hope of the Christian is that there is a good future ahead, though we may not see it—a future beyond the present suffering we are going through, and ultimately beyond this life. As Wiersbe continues,

> So when trials come, immediately give thanks to the Lord and adopt a joyful attitude. Do not pretend; do not try self-hypnosis; simply look at trials through the eyes of faith. Outlook determines outcome; to end with joy, begin with joy.[45]

This is real, tangible joy available to you in suffering, through Jesus Christ. From the standpoint of the non-Christian, joy in suffering may be an anomaly. Joy in life *generally* may be an anomaly for the non-Christian; and if that's true, then joy in suffering *specifically* must be an anomaly for the non-Christian. But for the Christian, joy can be the normal response. Why is this so, that Christians can "count it all joy"?

---

44. Wiersbe, *The Bible Exposition Commentary*, 338.
45. Wiersbe, *The Bible Exposition Commentary*, 338.

The Response to Suffering

The Gigantic Secret of the Christian

G.K. Chesterton shed light on why joy is possible for the Christian through all circumstances, including suffering. Chesterton said,

> It is said that Paganism is a religion of joy and Christianity of sorrow; it would be just as easy to prove that Paganism is pure sorrow and Christianity pure joy . . . Everything human must have in it both joy and sorrow; the only matter of interest is the manner in which the two things are balanced or divided . . . To the pagan the small things are as sweet as the small brooks breaking out of the mountain; but the broad things are as bitter as the sea . . . The mass of men have been forced to be gay about the little things, but sad about big ones. Nevertheless . . . it is not native to man to be so.[46]

In the balancing or dividing of joy and sorrow in your life, which one has the ascendancy? Are only the small things of life—the passing pleasures—giving you joy and sweetness? And are the broad things in life—the permanent, eternal pleasures—producing in you only sorrow and bitterness? If so, your life of joy and sorrow is lopsided or even upside down. If you "have been forced" to be happy about the small things, but are despondent about the grand scheme of life, you just may be living the life of an escapist. If sorrow in suffering, rather than joy, is the dominant theme of your life, no wonder you constantly want to escape suffering rather than endure—because who wants constant sorrow in a world of constant suffering? We humans want joy. Chesterton continued,

> Man is more himself, man is more manlike, when joy is the fundamental thing in him, and grief is superficial. Melancholy should be an innocent interlude, a tender and fugitive frame of mind; praise should be the constant pulsation of the soul . . . Joy ought to be expansive; but for the agnostic it must be contracted, it must cling to one corner of the world. Grief ought to be a concentration; but for the agnostic its desolation is spread through an unthinkable eternity . . . Joy, which is the small publicity of the pagan, is the gigantic secret of the Christian.[47]

The Christian can have joy through all circumstances in life, including suffering, because joy is part of what we possess at our core when we follow Jesus Christ. In the sense of being who God created us to be—joyful human

---

46. Chesterton, *Orthodoxy*, 241–2.
47. Chesterton, *Orthodoxy*, 241–2.

beings—we become "more manlike" when we follow the Son of God, Jesus Christ, who became the Son of Man.

Joy: the gigantic secret of the Christian! In actuality, it is a "secret" from the perspective of the non-Christian onlooker, but it is an openly known truth for the Christian. It is "gigantic" because it pervades, and ought to pervade, all of the Christian's life. But more importantly, God is the God of joy and he is joyful. God would have us receive of his joy and be joyful, both in suffering and out of suffering. What Chesterton is basically saying then is that, for the non-Christian, sorrow is the central experience of life and joy is peripheral. In contrast, for the Christian, joy is the central experience of life and sorrow is peripheral. They do coexist, yes, often lived out simultaneously or in alternation. But joy ought to, and does, dominate sorrow in the experience of the Christian.

The opportunities for joy to dominate sorrow abound. Every time we suffer and "consider it all joy," that central joy in suffering begins to push outward against the sorrow, like a growing baby pushes outward in her mother's womb. Eventually the central joy eclipses the peripheral sorrow until one day a person finds that there is no more suffering to be experienced. The birth pangs of earthly suffering have ended, and you are now in Heaven, where you can suffer no longer. The *practice* then for the joy of Heaven begins here on earth; we build such a central reserve of joy now that we become acquainted with the inexpressible joy that being in Heaven will give us one day. Joyful earthly living becomes a practice for, and a preview of, Heaven. As Warren Wiersbe said, "to end with joy, begin with joy."[48]

Making the Gigantic Secret Visible

But how, in practice, do our sufferings become opportunities for joy to dominate sorrow? How can we indeed learn to respond with joy in suffering and move closer to becoming endurance experts? In his famed poem—today a hymn sung to the motif of Beethoven's Ninth Symphony— Henry J. van Dyke wrote,

> Joyful, joyful, we adore Thee, God of glory, Lord of love;
> Hearts unfold like flowers before Thee, opening to the sun above.
> Melt the clouds of sin and sadness; drive the dark of doubt away;
> Giver of immortal gladness, fill us with the light of day!

---

48. Wiersbe, *The Bible Exposition Commentary*, 338.

The Response to Suffering

By the way, "immortal gladness" is a sound definition of joy, if you are looking for one. But the point here is that joy in suffering is available when we turn to this "Giver of immortal gladness," the Joy Giver, as a sunflower opens to the sun above. To make this idea—turning to the Joy Giver for joy in suffering—more practical, let's revisit the advice gleaned from King David in Chapter 2, tying his responses to suffering to this one considered here, *the* response of joy.

David's timeless advice for enduring suffering, from Psalm 55, is summed up in:

- Baring your heart and soul before God
- Pleading with God for justice
- Placing your confidence in God
- Encouraging other suffering people to do the same

When we bare the heart and soul *before God*, plead *with God*, and place our confidence *in God*, what we are doing is turning to God, the Joy Giver. When we encourage other people to do the same, we direct them to the Joy Giver. In following David's advice, rather than seeking to escape to our own little utopias, we are instead conversing with the God of this universe in our suffering. We are praying to God. In doing so, we are practicing that which will cause us to "consider it all joy when you encounter various trials," as James instructed his Christian readers. When we pray and converse with God, we are not only turning to God directionally, but we are entering his very presence. The Bible says, again in a Psalm written by King David, ". . . in your presence there is fulness of joy; at your right hand there are pleasures forever" (Psalm 16:11). He is not a God who is limited by location. He is omnipresent, present everywhere. He also is omniscient, having full knowledge—even of our suffering. So when we call upon him in prayer he listens, and we are spiritually in his presence, where there is fulness of joy.

Now in case all this is still a little ethereal for you, and you say, "I still don't see how praying to God in suffering is related to practically having joy in suffering," let me add this. The Lord Jesus knew we would feel that way. He knew we would crave joy in suffering, and it was Jesus Christ who established the connection between praying and receiving joy. In the Gospel according to John, Jesus promised,

> "Truly, truly, I say to you, if you ask the Father for anything in My name, he will give it to you. Until now you have asked for nothing in My name; ask and you will receive, so that your joy may be made full." (John 16:23–24)

Right there we see a more sure and practical connection between praying and receiving joy. Jesus himself desires that our central reserve of joy be made full, and desires for us to obtain joy by praying to the Father in Jesus' own name. As we pray in and through suffering, with time, practice, and experience, we will be able to "consider it all joy," and our joy will be "made full." With this we will not have to react to suffering, but will find ourselves, by and by, being able to rise above circumstances and rightly respond.

For the Christian who suffers, a metaphysical application of Newton's third law of motion will then read, "To every action there *does not have to be* an equal and opposite reaction. There *can be* an unequal and opportune response instead." And yet, when a response is required before the reasons for suffering are understood, it still leaves us asking the "Why?" question. We will look at the "whys" next.

Chapter 5

The Reasons for Suffering

IN PREMODERN TIMES, MOST people believed in absolutes. For some the sense of the absolute was founded on the supernatural; for others it was founded on the superstitious. But generally speaking, in premodern times, there was a recognition of absolute right and wrong. After premodern times though, there was a shift in what absolute beliefs were founded upon. The fall of the Bastille in France in 1789 is generally recognized by scholars as the historical landmark for the dawn of the modern era, which ended with the fall of the Berlin Wall in 1989.[49] Following the premodern era came the modern era, in which people still believed in absolutes, but for many, absolutes now had to answer to the rigid law of human reason.

The Enlightenment (roughly 1685–1815), which overlapped with the modern era, was ironically a period that produced great darkness across continental Europe, as hearts and minds were indoctrinated with naturalistic philosophy while biblical faith was largely abandoned. For the modernist, life had to be explained rationally and empirically. Anything perceived as inexplicable to human rationale and empiricism—including the historical, biblical tenets of the Christian faith—was dismissed as unacceptable. Historian Jonathan Hill notes that the European Enlightenment was "a grand experiment: the attempt to place Christianity on a solely rational footing"[50] (which he agrees failed). Hill continues,

---

49. Veith, *Post Modern Times*, 27.
50. Hill, *The History of Christianity*, 318–9.

> The question of what would replace it would be a key problem for the late eighteenth and nineteenth centuries—indeed it is a question for today.[51]

The replacement of the failed modernist Enlightenment philosophy is seen in the shift to postmodernism. Fed up with the rigidity and inability of a rationalism-only-approach to life's big questions, people abandoned *absolutes* and *reason*, turning instead to *relativism* and *irrationality*. People with a postmodernist worldview end up leaving life's great questions ultimately unanswered, as they suffer within suffering from a sense of utter meaninglessness and hopelessness. That's where many people find themselves today: without reasons for life, without meaning in suffering. It's not that *reason* or *reasons* have ceased to exist; rather it seems that *the postmodernist's desire* to seek reason and truth where it is evident and available *is dead*.

So too in suffering, many people would rather suffer in ignorance, never even attempting to find out why suffering exists so as to give it even an iota of meaning. As a result of a relativistic and irrational worldview, pain and suffering are easily dismissed as meaningless. In Chapter 2, I mentioned Richard Dawkins' view of suffering, which shows that postmodernist, naturalist philosophers such as he are not only apathetic in perceiving the reason for suffering, but are worse than sophomoric in explaining it. Again, Dawkins, who sees himself as a scientist, says of suffering and pain in the world,

> . . . some people are going to get hurt, other people are going to get lucky, and you won't find any rhyme or reason in it, nor any justice.[52]

Dawkins and those of his ilk see no rhyme or reason in suffering because they have abandoned or rejected the framework and foundation on which that rhyme and reason are built. Indeed, postmodernism is a philosophy that rejects frameworks and foundations, being rightly labelled "the worldview that denies all other worldviews."[53] Postmodernism is thus a self-refuting worldview.

God, however, has not left us with a worldview that denies reality. He has given us a realistic and ever-relevant view of the world and of life, even in and through suffering. We saw the Christian *response* to suffering in the

---

51. Hill, *The History of Christianity*, 318–9.
52. Dawkins, *A River Out of Eden*, 133.
53. Veith, *Post Modern Times*, 48.

previous chapter: counting it all joy, as we are drawn closer to God in our dependence on him. In this chapter, we explore the *reasons* for suffering and pain in the world in general, and more specifically in the life of the Christian, thus connecting it to the Christian response of joy.

The Reason for Suffering in the World

In our postmodern milieu, we as Christians do not seek *mere reasons*, either in life or in suffering. (To clarify, I use the word 'reason' in this context to mean 'root' or 'explanation,' and not 'purpose'). Reason for the sake of reason would be to revert to the modernist's failed experiment of removing God and the Bible from life and "the attempt to place Christianity on a solely rational footing." [54] Rather, we seek reason that is based on revelation. Our standard for *reason*, and in seeking *the reasons* for suffering, is that reason must have been revealed by God. Reason becomes evident once there is light. The light of God's Word, the Bible, is the only light that can make true reason evident, especially on the dark road of suffering.

What then is the reason for suffering in the world?

In his letter to the Romans, chapter 8, the apostle Paul wrote that all of creation—human beings and the ecosystems we inhabit—is suffering at the present. The Bible says,

> For we know that the whole creation groans and suffers the pains of childbirth together until now.
> (Romans 8:22)

Why is creation, and all of its components, groaning and suffering at this present time? In the sentence prior to the one above, Paul wrote,

> For the creation was subjected to futility, not willingly, but because of him who subjected it, in hope that the creation itself also will be set free from its slavery to corruption into the freedom of the glory of the children of God.
> (Romans 8:20–21)

Creation is groaning and suffering right now because it was subjected to "futility." The Bible says creation was subjected to futility because of "him," meaning God, who allowed this subjection or slavery to happen. In the beginning, when God created, creation was originally *free* and *permanent*

---

54. Hill, *The History of Christianity*, 318–9.

or eternal. But at some point in time, creation lost its freedom and permanence and became *enslaved* and *transient*. In fact, creation became enslaved *to* transience. That is, its free and eternal nature was revoked, and transience—the property of being vain or short-lived like a vapor—replaced it because corruption and decay set in.

But creation didn't just undergo this change by itself, by some sort of blind evolution. No. God caused his originally free and permanent creation to be enslaved to transience. God caused creation to be enslaved to decay, which ultimately leads to death. Creation is constantly under this curse of corruption (recorded in Genesis 3) that is moving toward death. This inherent corruption or death-nature that we see everywhere is why creation groans and suffers right now. This death-nature is the "futility" to which creation was subjected, which causes it, and us, to groan and suffer now.

So the shift in creation from permanence to transience didn't happen on its own, but because of God. But neither did God, the Creator, cause his creation to be enslaved to transience without good reason. It was *not* because God was feeling capricious or malevolent that he allowed creation to become enslaved to transience. No—it was because an element completely contrary to God's nature and purpose entered creation. What was that element which entered God's creation, and what was the conduit?

Paul explains, again in Romans,

> Therefore, just as through one man sin entered into the world, and death through sin . . . so death spread to all men, because all sinned.
>
> (Romans 5:12)

It was sin's entry into the world that caused God to allow his free and permanent creation to be enslaved to the transience and corruption that leads to death. The conduit through which sin entered the world was "one man," the historical Adam, the first created man. When Adam, part of God's free and permanent creation, disobeyed his Creator, sin entered the world. Once sin entered through Adam, all of his progeny since then—all of humanity—have been suffering and dying. We human beings are genetically predisposed to sin, and therefore to suffering and death. Sin is in our very blood. And suffering is in the very air we breathe. So then, if we trace the line for *the reason for suffering in the world* backward, it terminates at the point when sin entered the world through Adam.

The *reason* or *cause* then for suffering in this world is ultimately sin.

The *effect* of sin is suffering.

The Reasons for Suffering

Theologians refer to Adam's sin, which affects us all, as "original sin;" meaning that as Adam's children, every one of us is born into a state of sin, the effect of which is suffering. Even atheist Michael Ruse agrees in some part with this reason for suffering and death. Ruse says,

> I think Christianity is spot-on about original sin—how could one think otherwise, when the world's most civilized and advanced people (the people of Beethoven, Goethe, Kant) embraced that slime-ball Hitler and participated in the Holocaust?[55]

Why did the highly civilized and advanced Germans drink the escapist utopian Kool-Aid that Hitler served them? Because, as Aleksandr Solzhenitsyn rightly observed, "The line separating good and evil passes not through states, nor between classes, nor between political parties either, but right through every human heart, and through all human hearts."[56] We all feel the line that separates good and evil passing through our hearts. Every single human heart is sinful. Therefore we all commit evil acts from which we suffer in a world enslaved to decay, transience, and ultimately death. We all suffer because of the curse of sin, universal to all mankind. People suffer the effect of other people's sin. Still others suffer as result of their own sin.

Now, this may all seem very bleak and hopeless. And usually at this point in the discussion opponents of theism, and particularly of Christianity, will retort with something like, "If God exists, why does he allow evil?" Or simply "Why does God allow evil?" Apologist Clay Jones, as a follow-up question, responds brilliantly, "Why does God allow humans?"[57] That's a deeply searching question. We might even just stop at "Why does God allow?" If God knew we would suffer so much in this world which he himself caused to be enslaved to transience, he could very well have "not allowed" humans. Or God could have destroyed us when we first committed sin through Adam. Then none of us would be around to discuss sin, evil, or the reason for suffering, and everything would be better, right?!—Wrong, because *if God disallowed evil* in this world, there would be *no standard* to measure that "better" or good by! Also, *if God disallowed humans*, there would be *no one* around to complain about wanting things to be "better!" The animals, trees and rocks, though they groan, could not articulate their complaint verbally!

---

55. Jones, *Why Does God Allow Evil*, 42.
56. Solzhenitsyn, *The Gulag Archipelago*, 615.
57. Jones, *Why Does God Allow Evil*, 73.

The fact is, God has allowed humans. He has created us and allowed our existence despite our sin. Apologist Vince Vitale suggests that the answer to why God created human beings may be understood from the position of why human parents want to have children.

> ... the truth remains that by having a child, parents are doing something that they know will result in the child they procreate suffering death.... Why, then, do we think that having a child is morally permissible, and can even be loving and courageous? Because the child who comes to exist would not have existed otherwise.... similarly, in creating and sustaining this world rather than some other world, God bestowed on each of us not just any good, but the good of life.[58]

Most earthly parents understand the suffering involved in conceiving, bearing, and raising children. But they do it anyway, to give life. The Heavenly Father—God, the Creator—has created and continues to allow humans so that we may have "the good of life"—not without suffering, but through it. By way of analogy, God allowing creation and humans to exist, and our "allowing" children to exist through procreation, have this in common: the pains of childbirth. That's why in establishing that we do indeed suffer presently, Paul used the picture of childbirth:

> For we know that the whole creation groans and suffers *the pains of childbirth together until now.*
> (Romans 8:22)

In the case of a successful delivery of a baby, the pains of childbirth illustrate that suffering leads to life.

Therein lies the hope of creation: our present suffering is like childbirth, which after the pain of the birthing process has passed, yields a new life, a baby. So too, creation suffers, but "will be set free from its slavery to corruption into the freedom of the glory of the children of God" (Romans 8:21). This freedom will not come in some escapist utopia, but in the real Heaven that God is preparing for us. God still allows life now, in spite of suffering, but it is then that God will restore creation to its state of being *free* and *permanent*, from this current state of being *enslaved* and *transient*. Until then, we suffer as we experience the pains of childbirth.

---

58. Zacharias and Vitale, *Jesus among Secular gods*, 77.

The Reasons for Suffering

The Reason Christians Suffer

If sin is the reason for suffering in the world generally, is there any additional purpose the Christian suffers? Continuing on from the opening lines of James' letter to first-century Christians, introduced in Chapter 4, the Bible says,

> Consider it all joy, my brethren, when you encounter various trials, *knowing that the testing of your faith produces endurance.* (James 1:2–3)

Before I comment on the reason for the Christian's suffering, please notice something important in this passage from James: the expected *response* to suffering is stated before the *reason* for suffering in the life of the Christian is spelled out. This sequence is peculiar. If you prize logical progression, you may expect to have the reason before we can respond a certain way. But God, in his infinite wisdom, often deems it fit to write out the response he expects of us before he writes out reasons. We are asked to respond to suffering with joy before we know the reason for our suffering.

From this response-before-reason sequence emerges one way of conceptualizing what faith is. *Faith is responding to the circumstances of life as God expects, even before we know the reasons for those circumstances.* If we understand and experience faith in this way through suffering, we will not be tempted to acquiesce to an escapist worldview when a lack of reason bogs us down. Instead, we will focus on the response, knowing that the reason will come by and by, revealed in light of the response. As humans, most of us prize reason that leads to response; God prizes a response of faith that he uses to eventually lead us to reason—irrefutable and undeniable reason that will ultimately prove to be in accord with what God has revealed in his Word, the Bible.

With that said, there are two reasons or purposes God permits the Christian to suffer in this world of sin, according to this passage from James.

The Faith Reason

As the Christian responds to suffering with joy, we are told to recognize the fact that there is testing or a trial in process. We are being tested and tried by God. God is not just testing our character in general, but more specifically, God is testing our *faith,* which is the foundation of godly character:

> . . . *knowing that the testing of your faith* produces endurance.
> (James 1:3)

Why must God test the faith of a Christian? When you first become a Christian, your faith in Jesus is a faith for, or unto, salvation. If you are a Christian, as I am, it is that faith you and I placed in Jesus to save us from sin, straighten the Salvation in Circles road of escapism we were caught in, and liberate us with the truth so we could make onward progress. This faith is a gift of God's grace to us. After this initial faith is operative, the Christian must grow in Christlikeness: his or her faith in God must keep growing till it comes to resemble the perfect trust that Jesus had in his Father. The initial faith we place in God that leads to salvation is *a matter of a person trusting Jesus* to save him or her. The faith we place in God thereafter is *a matter of God trusting us* in the circumstances of life, including suffering. That's why he tests us, because, as Warren Wiersbe says, "a faith that can't be tested can't be trusted."[59] God does not need to test our faith due to a lack of knowledge about us on his part. He is omniscient. He tests us then not to get information, but to increase our intimacy with him.

The problem with the ancient Israelites in the wilderness was this: after God saved them from the Egyptians, they wanted to escape the wilderness of testing and return to Egypt. Their faith was not trustworthy in God's sight. Having gotten them out of Egypt, God then had to get Egypt out of them. God desires to bring us to a place where he is certain we will no longer look to escape his good ways and return to a life of sin. That's why God tests our faith in him, so that our faith in him is not just growing, but secure and unshakeable.

What, in God's eyes, is the mark of a secure, unshakeable, and trustworthy faith? This brings us to the second reason God permits the Christian to suffer in this world of sin.

The Endurance Reason

That second reason or purpose is so endurance can be produced in us through suffering:

> . . . knowing that the testing of your faith *produces endurance.*
> (James 1:3)

---

59. Wiersbe, *Be Available*, 58.

The Reasons for Suffering

We know we are learning to endure suffering when we no longer look to escape but instead trust God's divine design for the outcome, experiencing joy in suffering. In our experience, faith in God and endurance in suffering grow in tandem. We cannot have one without the other. While we endure, one of God's purposes in suffering—intimacy with himself—is being achieved. That is, when we endure suffering with joy, it is a mark of growing intimacy with God. It shows we are coming to know God so well that we can trust him with the suffering that comes from his hand and still stay committed to a relationship with him.

In fact, the Greek word for endurance has the connotation of "remaining under," implying the capacity to bear up under suffering.[60] In the Greek, the word translated "endurance" (*hypomene*) is a compound word composed of two simple words: *hypo*, which means "under," and *meno*, which means "to remain." In suffering, God desires for us to "remain under" the pressure and pain we feel until he accomplishes that which he purposes in us, through us, and for us. To endure suffering then means to remain under it and not escape, knowing it has come from the gracious hand of God. In the Introduction I said that none of us are, or will be, endurance experts on this side of eternity. That happens only once we cross the finish line of this race of life into Heaven. It will not happen in this life, because we will always have some form of suffering to remain under until the day we die, or until the day God makes all things new and opens Heaven to those who are his. Until then, we must "remain under."

Remaining under, then, is one of the purposes God has for suffering in the life of the Christian. If we seek to escape, we will be seeking to defeat God's purposes.

In my generation, we have a great need to learn what it means to remain under and be committed—to anything! In his book *After the Baby Boomers*, sociologist Robert Wuthnow says,

> . . . uncertainty, diversity, fluidity, searching, tinkering. The life worlds of young adults can be summarized in these words.[61]

Wuthnow's description is particularly apt when looking at the Millennial generation. Many of us lack the commitment to keep our word; some of us lack commitment in relationships; others lack commitment to finish what we have begun, and the list goes on. We are a generation that lacks

---

60. Louw and Nida, *Greek-English Lexicon* Vol. 1, 307.
61. Wuthnow, *After the Baby Boomers*, xvi-xvii.

the overarching quality of commitment, and as a result we suffer from uncertainty, diversity, fluidity, searching, and tinkering in life. The message of remaining under in suffering is not palatable for this generation—but it is a necessary message. For when we fail to learn to remain under the weight of suffering, we also fail to remain under or stay committed in other, lighter circumstances. That is why many of us remain stunted, not reaching the full potential God has for us.

When we seek an easy way out of suffering and escape through some alternate route, we become like the emperor moth that never flew. The emperor moth is a very beautiful creature after it emerges from its cocoon, glorious in flight with colorfully patterned wings. How the emperor moth comes to this regal state is instructive. The cocoon that houses the moth in its developmental stage is flask-like in shape. The insect must endure hours of intense struggle as it forces its way through the almost-impossible-to-get-through neck of the cocoon. Scientists who study insects explain that this pressure to which the moth is subjected works to force a life-giving substance into its wings, which strengthens it for flight. One day, watching the emergence of this creature from its cocoon, and wanting to lessen the moth's seemingly needless trial, Mrs. Charles Cowman decided she would give it a helping hand and lessen its struggle. With small scissors she snipped the restraining threads to make the moth's emergence painless and effortless. But sadly, as Mrs. Cowman put it, "My false tenderness had proved its ruin." [62] Giving the moth an 'escape' from its suffering deprived it of the strength it needed to fly. Instead, it spent its short life crawling painfully and pitifully instead of flying through the air on rainbow-colored wings.

Similarly, when we escape the pressures and pain of suffering God sends our way and seek release through human intervention, when we don't remain under that God-controlled pressure, we run the risk of not developing into the full-orbed person God intends for us to be. The ultimate example of that full-orbed person we seek to become like is Jesus Christ himself. God permits Christians to suffer for these reasons precisely because we are Christians, or Christ-followers. And as we follow Jesus, we will suffer as he suffered, so we may become like him. George MacDonald expressed it poignantly. He said,

---

62. Cowman, "Made Perfect Through Suffering."

The Reasons for Suffering

> The Son of God suffered unto the death, not that men might not suffer, but that their sufferings might be like his.[63]

Jesus did not suffer and die for us on the cross so that we could escape suffering and flee to our utopias on rosy beds of ease, but so that we would learn to respond to suffering like he did. Jesus' response to suffering is the ultimate pattern for us to follow as we suffer.

The Reason We Remain Under: Becoming Like Jesus

In a speech titled "Why are We Anti-Semites?" Hitler called Jews "criminals" and "parasites." Commenting on the need to exterminate them, he said,

> The heaviest bolt is not heavy enough and the securest prison is not secure enough that a few million could not in the end open it. Only one bolt cannot be opened—and that is death.[64]

On one point, Hitler was right—not about the Jews, but about death. The bolt of death cannot be opened . . . by man, that is. That's why Jesus came as a man. Jesus Christ came to open the bolt of death for mankind, for he alone holds the keys of death, as the Bible says in Revelation 1:18. The route Jesus took to open the bolt of death was by entering through the domain of our life into the domain of death. He provided a way out of suffering and death for those who believe on him—not by escaping, but by enduring his suffering even to death.

Only this pattern of Jesus will help us endure suffering and finally become endurance experts when we cross the finish line into eternity. There was only one human being who was an endurance expert on this earthly side of the finish line, and that was the Lord Jesus Christ. Yet even he had to pass through death before he became that endurance expert on this side of the finish line. That is why, in the book of Hebrews, the Bible instructs us who run the marathon race of life, to

> lay aside every weight, and the sin which so easily ensnares us, and let us run with endurance the race that is set before us, looking unto Jesus, the author and perfecter of our faith, who for the joy that was set before him endured the cross, despising the

---

63. MacDonald, *Unspoken Sermons*, 41.
64. Jones, *Why Does God Allow Evil*, 51.

shame, and has sat down at the right hand of the throne of God. (Hebrews 12:1–2, NKJV)

Since sin is the reason for suffering in the world, it easily ensnares and encumbers all runners in the marathon race of life. Therefore, we are told—as any wise running coach would instruct runners to get rid of unnecessary weight—to lay aside the weight of sin. Participating in the sin around us does not help us endure, but rather gives us impetus to escape and take our own path. To endure suffering well on the road to Heaven, the sin which permeates the entire created order and courses through our veins must be removed by Jesus. That is why we run this race of endurance *"looking unto Jesus."* He is our example for endurance.

There are three reasons why Jesus is our ultimate example in enduring suffering: His unrivaled qualification as Savior; his humiliation and joyful endurance; and his victory and exaltation.

His Unrivaled Qualification as Savior

The Bible says that Jesus is "the author and perfecter of our faith." He is the *author* of our faith because he gives us the gift of faith to trust him for salvation from sin and death. He also gives us the faith to overcome the presence and power of sin in this world as we suffer. He is the *perfecter* of our faith because through suffering, Jesus ensures our faith in him grows increasingly perfect as he tests us to the point of trustworthiness. Further, the faith that Jesus gives us works effectively to give us practical power over sin. Jesus validated his authorship of our faith by enduring death on the cross to save us from sin, and by rising from the dead. Therefore he alone is qualified to be our Savior.

In Chapter 1, I wrote that

> the notion of liberation demands that you need someone superior than yourself to free you from that which you could not resist being bound by in the first place and from that which you cannot save yourself now . . . not being able to save ourselves, we need a Savior who can bend the circular road to nowhere into a straight and narrow road which leads to light and liberty. . . . We need a Savior who can assure us that we have truly been saved in this life, and that the salvation will last beyond this life. And when this life has come to an end, we need a Savior who will safely escort

The Reasons for Suffering

us from this world to our final destination—that time and place where all suffering will have ended.

Jesus is that Savior.

In understanding Jesus' unrivaled qualification as Savior, we have to understand that Jesus was not held as you and I are by sin, which is the cause or *the reason for suffering* in this world. But even though he was born sinless and remained sinless throughout his life, Jesus nonetheless experienced *the effect of sin*—that is, suffering—and endured it. In his *humanity*, Jesus identified with the effect of sin; that is, suffering. In his *divinity*, however, Jesus remained above the cause or reason for suffering; that is, sin. So the Bible says that Jesus "was tempted in all things as we are, yet without sin" (Hebrews 4:15). All other saviors from among men—whether the Buddha, Hitler, or anyone else—have succumbed to sin and sinfulness. It is Jesus' absolute sinlessness that qualifies him, without rival, as the Savior of suffering sinners.

His Humiliation and Joyful Endurance

Jesus is not only the Savior of suffering sinners, but also the suffering Savior of sinners. This Savior, who is the author and perfecter of our faith, is the Savior "who for the joy that was set before him endured the cross, despising the shame . . . " For Jesus, there was joy in suffering under the will of God, his Father; and yes, the prospect of joy that lay beyond his death on the cross brought the presence of joy. But all this did not preclude his feeling pain and sorrow to the depth of his being. Far from it! Neither does the response of joy God expects of us in suffering preclude us from lamenting as we suffer. Joy and sorrow go together on the path of suffering and both are acceptable responses. In fact, both are needed, vital responses in order to suffer well. Even though he had joy, Jesus was not always upbeat and positive in his demeanor in a visible way. He did not refrain from lamenting.

In Isaiah 53, Jesus is referred to as a "man of sorrows." How then did he have simultaneous joy? For Jesus, the road through suffering was under-paved with joy, but also frequently potholed with lament and sorrow. There are multiple Scriptures—such as Matthew 17:14–17, Mark 7:34, Luke 22:44, and Hebrews 5:7–8 to name a few—that show the clear and vivid expression of Jesus' sorrow. For Jesus, the sorrow and pain he had in life were ultimately in view of the death he would die on the cross, where he would bear the sin of those who would believe on him. The joy was in view of that which lay beyond the cross: namely, our salvation being legally procured, and his resurrection from the dead. It is through the emotions of undergirding joy punctuated by sorrow that Jesus endured the cross to save us, despising the shame and ignominy it brought. Thus the great theologian B.B. Warfield would say of our Lord,

> When we observe him exhibiting movements of his human emotions, we are gazing on the very process of our salvation. . . . In his sorrow he was bearing our sorrows, and having passed through a human life like ours, he remains forever able to be touched with a feeling of our infirmities.[65]

Enduring suffering is an emotional endeavor that combines both an undergirding joy and an appropriately-expressed sorrow. Christian endurance in suffering is not the work of stoics who put on a stern face and never express joy or sorrow. I will say more about lament through suffering in the next chapter. Suffice it to say for now that Jesus expressed deep sorrow while enduring the humiliation of the cross and despising its shame.

Some of this sorrow he expressed while on the cross, where he experienced a range of sufferings, one of which was the suffering of separation. We hear his anguish when he cried out, "My God, my God, why have you forsaken me?" (Matthew 27:46). The eternal and hitherto unbroken bond of love between him and his Father seemed for a brief moment in time to be severed as sin was laid on him. He felt this separation and cried out in sorrow. The other kind of suffering Jesus experienced on the cross was the suffering of forgiveness. Jesus said, "Father, forgive them, for they do not know what they are doing" (Luke 23:34). There was suffering not just because of the public spectacle of crucifixion at the hands of the Romans, but more so because of the spiritual transaction of forgiveness occurring at that moment. Commenting on the suffering of forgiveness, Pastor Tim Keller says,

> Forgiveness means refusing to make them pay for what they did . . . to refrain from lashing out at someone when you want to do so with all your being is agony. It is a form of suffering. You not only suffer the original loss of happiness, reputation, and opportunity, but now you forgo the consolation of inflicting the same on them. You are absorbing the debt, taking the cost of it completely

---

65. Warfield, *The Person and Work of Christ*, 143–4

on yourself instead of taking it out of the other person. It hurts terribly. Many people would say it feels like a kind of death.[66]

For Jesus, it not only felt like death. It *was* death. In forgiving—and asking his Father to forgive—the sins of those who were crucifying him, and the sins of all who would believe on him, Jesus died. He absorbed the unpayable debt we owed God and took the cost of our offences against God—all our sin—completely upon himself. In passing through sorrows which only he could express, in forgiving us, and ultimately in dying for us, Jesus sets the pattern for enduring suffering that ends in victory and exaltation.

His Victory and Exaltation

In Hebrews 12:1–2, after telling us that Jesus is the author and perfecter of our faith who endured the cross, the writer goes on to say that Jesus "sat down at the right hand of the throne of God." But to get to that throne, Jesus had to first rise from the dead. And rise he did, as both the Bible and extrabiblical records testify through eyewitness accounts. Jesus Christ rose from the dead—victor over sin and death, conqueror of the grave. Yet to be victorious and conquer, Jesus had to pass through sin, suffering, and death, and endure it all. Commenting on Jesus' victory, Scottish preacher James S. Stewart powerfully wrote,

> He did not conquer in spite of the dark mystery of evil. He conquered through it.[67]

So must we. If we are to conquer the dark mystery of evil that currently shrouds all creation, we must conquer *through* it, and we must remain under the suffering it causes. And we can remain under suffering because Jesus did.

In a postmodern culture that shuns reason, we do not have to remain in the dark about the reason for suffering so that we lose meaning and hope. We may not have all the reasons on this side of eternity, but we have just enough from God in this life to give us hope, strength, meaning, purpose, joy, and much more in suffering.

---

66. Keller, *The Reason for God*, 196.
67. Stewart, *The Strong Name*, 55.

The reason for suffering in the world is sin. *The reason* or purpose why the Christian is permitted by God to suffer is so that the testing of our faith makes us people who endure, remaining under God-sent suffering. *The reason* the Christian can remain under suffering is because Jesus Christ, as our supreme example and inspiration, did. And while I have spelled out the reasons for suffering, let me add and underscore that the ultimate *purpose* (I am differentiating between reason and purpose here) for suffering in this world and in the life of the Christian is so that God may be glorified by it—so that he may be made much of—as he was glorified by the suffering and death of his Son Jesus Christ (John 17).

But the Christian faith is not just concerned with *responses* and *reasons* such as we've looked at thus far. We are also greatly interested in the *results* and *rewards* that follow right reasoning and responding. What are those rewards?

Chapter 6

The Rewards for Suffering Well

REWARD PROGRAMS ARE UBIQUITOUS today because of business strategy in a consumer-driven market. In an effort to invite customers and patrons to be loyal, businesses have created reward and loyalty programs, which do indeed achieve their purpose. This strategy of building customer loyalty through reward programs seems to be common to all businesses. Food stores, clothing retailers, banks and credit card corporations, airlines, coffee shops, and more—all cash in on this approach. And guess what? It works! Wouldn't you agree?

Sure, sometimes we may get fed up and withdraw from a certain program. But in general, who doesn't like to get cash-back rewards after months of paying off your credit card in a timely manner? Or who is opposed to getting a discount off a purchase of food or clothes after months, or maybe years, of sticking to the same grocery store or clothier? I'm not saying that this system is right or wrong, manipulative or pure in motive (although if reward programs are controlling you, that's surely a problem!). All I'm saying is that businesses strategically employ reward systems and consumers readily avail themselves of them.

What this concept of rewards in exchange for loyalty demonstrates is that commitment to a certain cause over the long haul, through thick and thin, pays off. Not just anyone is rewarded by a business, are they? Only registered and regular participants are rewarded. And not everyone is rewarded to the same degree. There are varying degrees of rewards, according to the degree of loyalty and investment.

God is merciful to offer rewards to those who suffer well, undeserving as we are. But God does have rewards for those he accepts into his plan of endurance—for those who respond with joy, remain under, and endure suffering under the kind hand of God. Having explored the *response to suffering* and the *reasons for suffering* in the previous two chapters, in this chapter I'd like to offer the Christian, biblical notion of *rewards for suffering well*.

We will find that unlike business rewards programs, God's "rewards program" never disappoints, but always exceeds our expectations. God asks us to remain under in suffering not to take something from us and leave us empty and hopeless, but to put something in us that was not there before, or to remake what was there.

Now let's suppose someone asked you to keep your head under water and remain under. Suppose they even tried to force you by holding your head under. It would be absurd to comply, because after a while you would remain under without coming back up! On the other hand, suppose a surgeon was working on a broken body part and told you to remain under his scalpel. It would be equally absurd if you refused. If you don't remain under the surgeon's corrective scalpel, you may escape for a while, but you will end up going right back under because you did not allow the surgeon to repair or remake what he was working on. To sum up the difference: remaining under water would be foolish; one must escape to save one's life. Remaining under the surgeon's scalpel would be wise; one must endure to save one's life. When God asks us to remain under in suffering, he does so to reward us and complete in us that which is lacking.

Before I touch on the right notion of rewards in suffering, I must set the context by contrast, and explore some wrong or perhaps skewed notions people have of rewards in life and in suffering. In Chapter 1 I said I would comment here on certain so-called Christian camps that have an escapist rather than an endurance outlook in suffering. No surprise, the *zeitgeist* of escapism prevalent in the world has subtly crept into the Church. What are these Christianized forms of escapism, and what accounts for them?

Rewards Without Right Reasoning: Failed Christian Attempts to Complete an Incomplete Life

When we experience suffering and pain, what we seek most is for the broken parts of our life to be made whole, and the incomplete parts of our life to be made complete. In his classic work *The Problem of Pain*, C.S. Lewis wrote,

> Now error and sin both have this property, that the deeper they are the less their victim suspects their existence; they are masked evil. Pain is unmasked, unmistakable evil; every man knows that something is wrong when he is being hurt.... Pain insists on being attended to. God whispers to us in our pleasures, speaks in our consciences, but shouts in our pain: it is his megaphone to rouse a deaf world.[68]

"Pain *insists* on being attended to." That which is broken cries to be fixed; that which is incomplete cries for completion. God allows this so that we will turn to him to be healed and be made complete. What's interesting is that while most human beings do well at recognizing pain and suffering (unless they suffer from a condition such as congenital insensitivity to pain[69], mentioned at the start of Chapter 2), many are prone to fail at rightly attending to the pain and suffering we recognize. That is, we attend to it on our own and do not rightly respond to the call that comes through God's megaphone. We have the propensity to turn to manmade substitutes, routes of escape that call to us from man's "mini-phones," instead of heeding God's megaphone.

In some so-called churches and Christian circles, God's megaphone is stopped up, and man's mini-phones are played at blaring volumes while people suffer. These camps offer various forms of "Christianized escapism." I would like to highlight three forms of Christianized escapism, the first two of which are well known by their tags: the positivity gospel and the prosperity gospel. The third I call "the painless programs gospel." I realize I could also write about the social justice gospel and other perversions of the true gospel, but for our purposes, I'll stick to these three.

The Positivity Gospel

The concept of positive thinking as the path to a successful Christian life may have existed prior, but was made famous through the life and work of Norman Vincent Peale. Peale wrote many books, perhaps the most notable of which is 1952's *The Power of Positive Thinking*. The title says much: think

---

68. Lewis, *The Problem of Pain*, 89–94.
69. Connor, "The People Who Can't Feel Pain."

positively about everything, and you will have power. The question of suffering then—with its bare human pain—is never faced squarely, because it is something negative that must be escaped. In order to achieve power through positive thinking, Peale twisted Scripture to fit his agenda, fusing it with techniques from psychoanalysis. For example, in writing about prayer, Peale introduced formulas of prayer such as "Prayerize-Picturize-Actualize."[70] Misapplying Scriptures such as Matthew 18:19 and Mark 11:24, he said that if you pray about something, imagine it in your mind, and assume it will come true, it will indeed come true. Nothing is said about God, through Jesus Christ, as the object as of our faith. It is all about the self taking control of one's destiny. If you'll indulge me here, I agree with whoever compared the apostle Paul with Peale and said, "I find Peale appalling, and Paul appealing!"

Appalling as Peale's worldview was, other Christian ministers followed in his positive thinking train. Robert Schuller was well known for his *Hour of Power* television program, in which he preached a slightly different packaging of Peale's positivity message, but the content was essentially the same. It's well known that Schuller would say erroneous things like Jesus "met needs before touting creeds."

Today, the mantle of positivity thinking in America is worn by Joel Osteen. Though he seems to try hard to be balanced, Osteen still ends up preaching a positivity message that inspires people to live *Your Best Life Now*—the title of one of Osteen's most popular books. My humble question is, "If one's best life is *now*, what about Heaven? Will it be any *better* there?" Osteen does address the question of suffering. However, his explanation of how to respond to suffering is veneered over with the positivity gospel message, at the expense of seeking answers from a *primarily* Christian, biblical framework.

For example, Osteen says that in trials God is "trying to shape you into the person he wants you to be."[71] That's partially true. In suffering, God *is* shaping us. The error lies in the idea of God "trying." Since when does God *try* to do anything? Osteen also encourages readers who are going through trials to not "give up. Don't quit. Don't whine and complain, saying, 'God, why is all this happening to me?'"[72] Why not complain to God in suffering? Can God not take it? What about David pouring out his heart

---

70. Peale, *The Power of Positive Thinking*, 60.
71. Osteen, *Your Best Life Now*, 206.
72. Osteen, *Your Best Life Now*, 211.

in complaint to God in the Psalms, such as what we considered in Chapter 2? Osteen does not call for endurance founded *exclusively* on the Word of God, through the power of the Holy Spirit, by which Jesus Christ is exalted in our lives in a sin-sick world. So as well-intentioned as Osteen may be, it turns out in the end to be a soft form of escapism.

You say, "Why are you being so negative about people who are trying to be positive?" Well, first of all, I'm not saying we should not be positive. Of course we should be positive. That's part of a life of faith in Christ. In his letter to the Philippians, Paul taught,

> Finally, brothers, whatever is true, whatever is honorable, whatever is just, whatever is pure, whatever is lovely, whatever is commendable, if there is any excellence, if there is anything worthy of praise, think about these things. (Philippians 4:8)

That's true positive thinking, and it has power. But, you see, a battery has a positive *and* a negative terminal. We need both for power to come out of the battery. Paul's positivity, as opposed to Peale's, is well-grounded because he reasons through the negative in life before making assertions about the positive. That's realistic. That helps us to rightly respond to suffering. To talk only about the positive, as if life has nothing negative or that the negative can be escaped or controlled by us, is illusory. Sadly, these positivity gospel camps do just that. They encourage people to seek rewards without rightly responding to suffering and long before the race of endurance has been run. Thus whatever is incomplete in a suffering person remains incomplete, because only God can complete it, in his way.

The Prosperity Gospel

Another seemingly rewarding spin on the gospel, one that really seeks to complete the incomplete parts of life—especially an incomplete bank balance—is the prosperity gospel. Proponents of the prosperity gospel focus on getting wealth, material possessions, and health. They teach essentially that since Jesus died to set us free from sin, part of that deal is our having phenomenal success in these areas. The way out of suffering then is the path to more riches, possessions, and health. According to them, if you don't have these things, you are probably in sin or don't have enough faith. How interesting that these rich preachers prey on poor and suffering people with their message!

There are many well-known prosperity gospel preachers who are known to have unrealistic, utopic, and escapist views of life and suffering. They are also known to make outrageous requests of their followers. For example, prosperity gospel preacher Jesse Duplantis recently asked his followers to consider donating $54 million towards the purchase of a Falcon 7X jet plane.[73] As of this writing, Duplantis already owns three private jets. He claims that God himself told Duplantis to "believe" him for this fourth one, which would be an "upgrade." And why does Duplantis need this fourth jet?—So that as he goes around the world preaching the (prosperity) gospel, he can be higher up and closer to God in prayer. So much for preachers of the true gospel of Jesus Christ who suffer with broken backs yet have been crisscrossing the globe for the major part of their adult lives, flying on commercial airliners, never entertaining the thought of asking for a personal private jet, because it would bring ill repute to the name of their Lord and Master, Jesus Christ.

What proponents of the prosperity gospel are blind to is the fact that rewarding ourselves with earthly riches will never complete the incomplete in us. It will never help us endure suffering rightly. Job, the biblical hero of the faith, who suffered beyond expression but responded rightly to suffering, was a rich man. Yet he said, "Naked I came from my mother's womb, and naked I shall return" (Job 1:21). Solomon, one of Israel's richest and wisest kings, said of rich people, "As he had come naked from his mother's womb, so will he return as he came. He will take nothing from the fruit of his labor that he can carry in his hand" (Ecclesiastes 5:15). We may have riches while we run the race of life, but it is certain we will carry nothing with us when we cross the finish line into eternity. That ought to be a clue that riches can neither ultimately satisfy, nor help us endure suffering. But prosperity gospel preachers don't practice these tried and true biblical principles. Why not?

It has to do with the fact that they do not understand what the true gospel *is* and what it *is not*. If their gospel can put food into someone's belly but cannot save their soul, it is not the true gospel. If their gospel can relieve racial tension and bridge ethnic divides but cannot unite people of different ethnicities into the one people of God, purchased by the blood of Jesus, it is not the true gospel. If their gospel can infuse a person with a positive attitude to life but can give him no power over sin, it is a false gospel. If their gospel can take a person from rags to riches in this world but leave

---

73. Wootson Jr., "A televangelist wants his followers."

her impoverished in the world to come, with no inheritance in Christ, it is a false gospel. If their gospel can organize and entertain, without convicting or giving hope in pain, it too is a false gospel.

It shouldn't surprise us, though, that the proponents of both the positivity and prosperity gospels don't really understand what the true gospel is—that it is *the* good news in the context of bad news. It is that good news about the person of Jesus Christ, about his cross and resurrection; about the Creator and Owner of the universe relinquishing his heavenly position to become the poor and powerless God-Man; about our sin and salvation, Heaven and Hell; and about our enduring the suffering of this life, by faith, as we wait in preparation for the reward of Heaven. That's what the gospel is. But better than my definition, Paul said this, under the inspiration of the Holy Spirit:

> I am not ashamed of the gospel of Christ, for it is the power of God to salvation for everyone who believes, for the Jew first and also for the Greek.
> (Romans 1:16, NJKV)

Prosperity and positivity gospel preachers are not attracted to this power of which Paul writes. They are ashamed of it. But they are attracted to earthly power, because they have allowed a certain strain of the postmodern virus into their thinking. Christian philosopher Gene Edward Veith, Jr. says,

> Since postmodern thought is impatient with transcendent spiritual beliefs, the focus shifts to the here and now, to the tangible. People have little interest in Heaven; they want health and wealth now. *Since postmodernists are oriented to power,* they will be drawn to power churches which promise miracles to solve every problem, political clout, exponential numerical growth, and success after success.[74] (Emphasis mine)

Remember, the postmodern spirit eschews reasoning and follows relativism and irrationality. So positivity or prosperity gospel preachers and their followers can still put themselves under the Christian banner, yet excuse themselves from fully following biblical, historical Christian doctrine and practice, choosing those parts that fit their fancy. They seek then—albeit in futility—to reward themselves with power through riches

---

74. Veith, *Post Modern Times*, 213.

and success, remaining incomplete through suffering, because only God can complete what is incomplete in us, in his way.

The Painless Programs Gospel

A third form of Christianized escapism that people are exposed to, albeit very innocuously, is the "painless programs gospel." It's a sad thing because it's so pervasive in American and global evangelicalism, yet not many people recognize it as harmful. It is not as overt as the positivity and prosperity gospels. What exactly is the painless programs gospel?

As the name suggests, it seeks to sell Christianity and Church life as painless and full of programs. That is, pain is shunned or not talked about, and a spiritual diet of fun, lightness, ease, and warm fuzzy programs—bereft of truth on the heavy issues—becomes the staple of Church life. None of these things are wrong *per se*, but as the staple they leave the Christian stunted and incomplete.

Commenting on what the Church's response to suffering ought to be, Christian philosopher Alvin Plantinga says, "Such a problem calls, not for philosophical enlightenment, but for pastoral care."[75] What a wise and discerning word! But the issue we face in evangelicalism in handling the problem of pain and suffering is that there is a pastoral carelessness at the popular, public level. Not that all pastors are careless in handling the issues of pain and suffering. No. There are wise and caring shepherds who are in tune with the suffering of their flock. I know many personally. What I am commenting on, however, is the broadly general attitude and atmosphere of evangelicalism, particularly in church settings where there is a shallowness and superficiality in services and other intimate settings, settings where suffering is shunned. In his book *Between Pain and Grace,* Andrew Schmutzer points out,

> People with hearts crippled with profound pain are forced to stand up and clap week after week with little if any mention of the dark trials that fill their hearts. . . . Wounded people among us 'smell' the pretense that is as programmed and insincere as the canned laughter of sitcoms. They are correct. Shunned grief is spiritual hypocrisy.[76]

---

75. Zacharias and Vitale, *Jesus among Secular gods*, 27.
76. Schmutzer and Peterman, *Between Pain and Grace*, 105.

In other words, there is no room for grief or lament. Have you been in church services or other settings like this which are performance-like and programmatic? Authenticity is lacking. I know of people who find it unbearable if there is simply a song in their church service in a minor key, as if all of life were written in a major key. Minor-key moments are meant to highlight the sorrows, griefs, and sufferings of life, so we can better connect to and appreciate the joy of the major-key moments. The joy brought by praising God in the major key is attractive. But in a world of suffering, lament over sin and brokenness in the minor key is necessary. Again, Schmutzer says,

> If the performance of praise exalts and affirms, the performance of lament names and transforms. Without pain, praise is 'thin' and halfhearted; but without praise, the pain seems fatal and unbearable.[77]

There must be a balance then in the tangible expression of joy and sorrow, and this happens in a constant and growing relationship with Jesus Christ. Perhaps for some Christians, deep transformation is lacking because they have not yet learned to lament over sin and suffering. Pastors need to realize this and teach it. The Old Testament prophets taught it, and so did the New Testament apostles. God, through the prophet Jeremiah, cried out against the pastors of Israel saying, "They have healed the brokenness of My people superficially, Saying, 'Peace, peace,' But there is no peace" (Jeremiah 6:14). If Christians today—Christians in Western, American evangelicalism—don't learn, and if pastors and preachers don't teach their people to face suffering as our Lord did, we will remain incomplete and consequently unrewarded as we suffer.

Against the backdrop of those wrong or skewed notions of rewards in suffering, I want to now touch on the Christian, biblical notion of rewards in suffering.

The Right Rewards: Completing the Incomplete

If *joy* is the Christian's *response to suffering*; if *sin* is the *reason for suffering* in the world; if *the reason a Christian suffers* is so that *the testing of our faith produces endurance*, what then is *the reward for suffering well*? Continuing the opening lines of James' letter to first-century Christians—from which

---

77. Schmutzer and Peterman, *Between Pain and Grace,* 108.

we have so far drawn the response and reasons for suffering in Chapters 4 and 5—the Bible then says,

> And let endurance have its perfect result,
> so that you may be perfect and complete, lacking in nothing.
> (James 1:5)

These first-century Christians were to endure suffering because whatever was incomplete in them as Christians was being completed. In the persecution they underwent—being maligned verbally, attacked physically, and even put to death—these Christians, who were suffering for the cause and the name of Jesus Christ, were being perfected; that is, they were being made more like Jesus as they endured.

The same applies to us today. When you suffer under the hand of God, whatever is lacking in you is being supplied by God. As he works to perfect the imperfect and complete the incomplete, God is not just modifying our outward behavioral patterns so we behave better on the other side of suffering, like someone whose behavior changes out of sheer terror for a tyrant. God is not after mere outward behavioral change. Rather, he is bringing us to a place of loving him with all our heart, mind, soul, and strength. He is remaking us from the inside out, into completely different people. So C.S. Lewis said,

> And that is why tribulation cannot cease until God sees us remade
> or sees that our remaking is now hopeless.[78]

It is better for us to be remade under the hand of God than to be left completely hopeless by constantly trying to escape from him in suffering. When we endure suffering, God fills the lacunae he sees in our personality, in our character, and most importantly in our likeness to his Son Jesus Christ. This is the "perfect result" of endurance James writes of: it completes the Christian. It is in order to receive *this reward* that we should remain under suffering—the reward of being remade, being completed and perfected by God to become more like his Son, Jesus Christ. To become more and more like Jesus is a reward beyond what we deserve. Our reward is not a perfect prize or position in this life after we have suffered, but that we ourselves are the prizes of God he is working on. He prizes us who believe in his Son Jesus Christ, just as he prizes his perfect and complete Son.

---

78. Lewis, *The Problem of Pain*, 107.

The Rewards for Suffering Well

Jesus Christ was and is the perfect man: there was not a single imperfection in his character, and that is still the case. Jesus Christ was and is the complete man: there was not an incomplete facet about him, and that is still true. He lacked nothing, absolutely nothing (except sin), and he lacks nothing today. And yet remember, Jesus was the God-Man: fully God *and* fully man, the Son of God *and* the Son of Man. That means the suffering he endured did have the effect of perfecting something on the human side of his nature. The Bible says,

> Although he was a Son, he learned obedience from the things which he suffered. And having been made perfect, he became to all those who obey him the source of eternal salvation.
> (Hebrews 5:8–9)

Not that Jesus Christ had any sin, but rather that as the *Son* of God, as a human, even Jesus had to learn obedience to the will of the Father. It is in this sense that he was perfected, in learning obedience to the Father through suffering. Obedience was central to Jesus' endurance. And if Jesus, who was *already perfect as the Son of God*, had to learn obedience to be *perfected as the Son of Man*, how much more do you and I? Obedience to God the Father is central to our enduring suffering. And obedience to God is *always* rewarding, just as obedience to earthly parents is rewarding.

In God's rewards program, there are three aspects to rewards when we suffer well: immediate, eventual, and eternal rewards.

Immediate Rewards

God does not hold all rewards till later. There is incentive as soon as we enter into a season of suffering. Before James told his readers they were being perfected and completed in suffering, when first telling them the reason for their suffering, he said something very enlightening:

> . . . knowing that the testing of your faith produces endurance.
> (James 1:3)

The word "knowing" is key here. When we enter suffering, we are able to respond with joy and endure because we *know* that God is testing our faith to produce endurance. Knowing that we are being tested by God is an immediate thing, contiguous with recognizing the reality of the suffering we are in. It is a reward indeed that God allows us to "know," or be aware of, not only the fact that we are suffering, but that in the suffering he is at work. This knowledge given to us in suffering is an immediate reward we should thank God for. We not only know that God is testing our faith, but we also begin to know ourselves in suffering. When we are sorely pressed by the pressures of suffering, what's in our hearts begins to come out as we either react or respond. There's nothing like the crucible of suffering to reveal who we really are.

Millennials often seek to complete the incomplete in us with the help of personality tests and personality types. There is a great fascination with these tests and types in my generation, because we desperately want answers to the question, "Who am I?" There are some helpful personality tests such as the Enneagram, Myers-Briggs, DISC, and many more. However, as helpful as these may be, they cannot ultimately tell you who you really are. Only God can do that, for he has created us. God employs the crucible of suffering to give us the knowledge of who he is, of who we are, and of his work to bridge the gap between the two.

Eventual Rewards

While God rewards us immediately in suffering with the knowledge that he is testing us, there are some rewards he holds back till later. The actual completing of the incomplete in us is an eventual reward, something we are given by and by. When James says "let endurance have its perfect result, so that you may be perfect and complete, lacking in nothing" (James 1:5), the perfecting of the imperfect and the completing of the incomplete is clearly *God's part to perform*. It is an eventual reward in the sense that it comes as we continue enduring the marathon race of suffering in life. It requires waiting. It is also eventual in the sense that it pertains to this earthly life, happening at a point in time removed from when we enter into a season of suffering. In every season of suffering, we may be sure that there is something incomplete God is completing in us, some imperfect facet in the diamond of our character that God is better shaping and polishing to his standard, so that his glory may be displayed in and through us. Again, this is God's part in rewarding us.

But there is also a responsibility we have. In order to receive this eventual reward of being made complete, we must allow or "let" endurance have its perfect result. In other words, we are not to escape or give up prematurely. We must allow God to work on us. God will never force his perfecting work

The Rewards for Suffering Well

upon us, even in the suffering he allows under his sovereignty. We need to allow him to work, submitting to him in trust that he is indeed cutting and polishing our imperfect facets, like a lapidary working on a diamond. Many Christians scarcely receive this eventual reward of being completed because they simply do not allow God to work on them; they seek to escape his gracious hand by running away, keeping busy, or covering their lives with substitutes that give the appearance of being complete.

Are you allowing endurance to have its perfect result, so that you are perfect and complete, lacking in nothing?

If we were to think of endurance and our being made complete from the viewpoint of a little piece of coal—imagining it to be a sentient piece of coal—it might help us see the eventual reward of being complete in better light. (Note: although nature's actual process in forming a diamond involves a dense piece of carbon different from coal, I'm calling it a piece of coal here for the sake of simplicity.)

Imagine with me that deep inside the earth there lived a little piece of coal, surrounded by much larger pieces. As you know, as one goes deeper into the earth's crust, temperatures get hotter and hotter, and the pressure gets higher and higher. It feels like you have the whole world on top of you! Well, as the years passed, this little piece of coal began feeling the pressure of living so deep in the earth under such high temperatures. He said, "Let me just give up. I will presently crumble to powder, and it will all be over."

As time went on, the coal also found himself moving away from the crust of the earth, being pushed deeper and deeper, so that eventually he ended up in the earth's mantle. Again, the piece of coal wanted to give up. But then he began to see something. Over the years, the other, larger pieces of coal around him in the earth's mantle gradually began to develop a sheen. They were being transformed. "Wow," said the little coal, "I want to shine like them too!" This little one was given strength and resolve to continue, and as the years passed, he increased in size. The deeper into the earth he was pushed, the greater the pressure and the higher the temperatures became. Many times he thought of escaping it all and simply crumbling to powder. Now, though, he'd become so strong that he couldn't crumble even if he wanted to! What's more, he and his fellow coals started to notice that he now had a certain shine to him. This encouraged him. He continued to persevere, and very soon his light, black, opaque body became shiny, heavy, and translucent.

More years passed, until one day diamond miners dug deep into the earth. They mined coal, stones, and debris. Among the detritus was a large stone: heavy, beautiful, and bright. It almost blinded one miner when he lifted it up to the sunlight. The little piece of coal had become large, brilliant, and sparkling—no longer coal, but transformed into a diamond. The diamond was taken to a jewel shop, cut, polished, and refined by the lapidary. Very soon, a king's personal jeweler heard of it and sought to add this diamond to his king's crown. From deep in the hot, pressurized earth, there sat our little coal atop the crown of a king—now a diamond shining with beauty and radiance, into which light could enter and radiate outward to be seen by the whole world.

By way of analogy, so it is with us. Christians who suffer are like pieces of dense carbon under pressure, who God transforms into diamonds fit to be displayed in his own jewel collection. God is the divine Lapidary who works on us. He, as it were, forms us in the earth, mines us out, cuts and polishes us until we are perfect and complete, lacking nothing, so that the light and love of Christ can shine in and through us the more we endure suffering. Thus, we are rewarded eventually with the likeness of his own nature as we endure on this side of eternity.

Eternal Rewards

When we cross the finish line into eternity, that's where—if I may say so—the "real" rewards for having endured earthly suffering begin. Any reward we receive from God on this side of the finish line is but a preview of the eternal rewards we will receive. The endurance we build up in suffering here on earth catapults us into eternity as conquerors. We conquer not because we are strong, proud, or brilliant on our own; that's the illusion of our culture. Rather, we conquer in this life and into eternity because we are weak, humiliated, and lacking wisdom of our own, so that only in Christ are we able to conquer. Jesus is the pioneer of moving from earthly endurance to spiritual victory, conquering both in this life and into eternity. As Clay Jones puts it,

> Jesus knew that to conquer in the spiritual realm he had to suffer in the physical realm and so he allowed himself to suffer humiliation, excruciating torture, and death.[79]

---

79. Jones, *Why Does God Allow Evil*, 194.

The Rewards for Suffering Well

Jesus allowed himself to suffer on earth, entering into the domain of our life and then into the domain of death, where he conquered both death itself and that spiritual being who temporarily held power over death. Why did Jesus enter the domain of human life and then enter the domain of human death? The Bible says,

> that through death he might render powerless him who had the power of death, that is, the Devil . . .
> (Hebrews 2:14b)

Through his suffering on the cross which caused him to enter the domain of death, Jesus defeated the Devil, conquered death, and forever has power over death. He is the Master of death, able to take death away from those who believe in him and grant us eternal life. It is because Jesus demonstrated obedience in enduring the cross, conquering death and the Devil, that the Bible further says,

> For this reason also, God highly exalted him, and bestowed on him the name which is above every name, so that at the name of Jesus every knee will bow of those who are in heaven and on earth and under the earth, and that every tongue will confess that Jesus Christ is Lord, to the glory of God the Father.
> (Philippians 2:9–11)

What a reward this was given to Jesus by God, his Father—an eternal reward! Today, Jesus is exalted *eternally*, never to suffer or die again. In his eternally exalted state, Jesus reigns over the universe. One day soon, everyone—with absolutely no exceptions—will bow to the kingship of Jesus Christ. All of this because, in obedience to God, Jesus endured suffering. And to those of us who endure, the conditional promise is given,

> If we endure, we will also reign with him . . .
> (2 Timothy 2:11–14)

This is just one of the many eternal rewards promised to us for enduring—reigning with Jesus Christ as co-regents over the heavens and the earth. Another eternal reward worth mentioning again, previously mentioned in Chapter 4, is " . . . in your presence there is fulness of joy; at your right hand there are pleasures forever" (Psalm 16:11). All the utopias and kingdoms people sought to build and reign over on earth in a bid to escape suffering will be shown to be futile and illusory when conquering Christians reign with their conquering King, Jesus Christ.

If you are a Christian who is suffering, why not take some time to come before God and take inventory of your life in light of eternity?

- How are you doing in responding to God in your suffering?
- Are you responding with joy?
- Are you trusting God by remaining under, and seeing the test of your faith produce more endurance in you?
- Are you seeing immediate and eventual rewards from God being borne out?
- Are you working to build up eternal rewards as you endure?

You do not want to cross the finish line into eternity only to find that your rewards are a paltry sum, do you? We would all do well to pray to God like the great American theologian and philosopher Jonathan Edwards did in his teenage years: "Stamp eternity on my eyeballs."

More Rewards: Heavenly Wisdom for Earthly Endurance

What if you are not doing so well in responding to suffering? None of us, irrespective of our levels of suffering, are equipped enough or intelligent enough to navigate the various components of suffering caused by sin in this world. That is why God's rewards program has an added bonus, so to speak, a highly critical component required to suffer well. James continues to instruct his first century Christian readers to endure suffering on their way to being made complete by God, saying,

> But if any of you lacks wisdom, let him ask of God, who gives to all generously and without reproach, and it will be given to him. (James 1:5)

Here is the offer of heavenly wisdom to endure earthly trials. If we lack wisdom—and the starting point of gaining it is to admit that we do lack—we may ask God. God promises to give wisdom to the suffering man or woman who asks him for it. We may not be given all the reasons for suffering and evil on this side of eternity, but God will give us the wisdom we require: the light to tread the darksome and convoluted path of sin and suffering so that we endure with joy, and having endured, arrive at the finish line ready to cross into eternity. Either we can ask God for his wisdom, and he will give it, or we can continue in folly with the ways of the world in dealing with suffering. But we cannot have God's ways commingled with man's ways. That's why James goes on to comment on the manner of our asking for wisdom in suffering,

> But he must ask in faith without any doubting, for the one who doubts is like the surf of the sea, driven and tossed by the wind. (James 1:6)

We can conclude there is no God, becoming wise in our own eyes, never seeking God's wisdom. Worse, knowing fully well that God exists, we can still be wise in our own eyes. In both cases we will make escape routes of our own in suffering instead of asking God for wisdom. The more sensible option is to believe that God is, and to have faith that he rewards us with wisdom in suffering when we ask. This is more sensible, because all other escape routes terminate in dead ends with no answers. Only with God is there an open door of hope at the end of the road.

In Chapter 1, I wrote about the doctrine of Salvation in Circles, referring to the growth of Buddhism and similar Eastern religions in the West. I said that the *reason* for this circular notion of salvation is that they believe there is no God to call us to account. Since there is no God to call us to account or save us, the *result* is that we must save ourselves. But since in reality we cannot be our own saviors, ultimately, we must look to escape everything life throws our way—especially suffering. I also said, having given the *reason* and *result* of this circular notion of salvation, that I would give *a sensible response* to this erroneous notion, a response that will help straighten the circular path and save the helpless hamster from senselessly running on the wheel to nowhere! What is that sensible response that people locked in the circular salvation ruts of Buddhism, Hinduism, and other systems need to consider?

The sensible response to the Salvation in Circles notion is to take up the offer of heavenly wisdom that the God of the Bible gives. When you are driving somewhere and get lost, what do you do? You either ask a real person or rely on your GPS for directions. You do not rely on your own wisdom when you are lost, do you? If you had wisdom of your own, you wouldn't be lost in the first place. God has given us who are lost in a world of suffering the option of asking him for directions, for his wisdom. We would be foolish not to do so! Anyone can ask God for wisdom. Granted, in its context this promise is given to suffering Christians; however, even if you are not a Christian, you can still ask God for wisdom. Of course, the first piece of wisdom God will undoubtedly give you is to believe in his Son, the Lord Jesus Christ, as your Savior, who will set you free from the circular rut of sin and self-saving you are stuck in. After you believe in Jesus and have enrolled in God's rewards program, the wisdom of God available to you is inexhaustible; he will never deny your request for wisdom, giving you guidance tailor-made for your situation. But you must believe in Jesus first.

To those of us who have believed in Jesus Christ, we must continue believing him in our suffering. We must ask for his wisdom, which will help us stay on the straight and narrow path and will help us avoid the circular paths of escapism. And we know when we ask, he will give us the wisdom we need. We have the privilege to ask today, because there is coming a day when we will not need to ask God for wisdom to suffer well. In this earthly life of endurance, we are traveling to Heaven, where no suffering will exist. But we need wisdom now to get to Heaven in a manner that pleases God and prepares us for that world.

What will that world with no suffering be like? In wrapping up this journey toward becoming endurance experts, I invite you to consider the reward of Heaven.

Chapter 7

The End of Suffering: When East and West Converge

"The End"—words we usually hear or read when there's nothing more to be had from a storybook or play. The words used to appear onscreen in movies or television programs after all the credits had rolled, to signal that there was nothing to watch beyond that point. Technical reasons and trends apart, I wonder if "The End" appears less often nowadays because of the desire which viewers and content creators have for continuity or permanence. In other words, by not using "The End," could authors and directors be communicating that the story is not supposed to end? Maybe. I'm not sure. What I do know is that sometimes we feel a tinge of sadness when "The End" comes. Other times "The End" can't come soon enough. And whether or not you want something to end normally depends on the pleasure or pain you experience, doesn't it?

Regardless of how we feel about endings, the truth is that not only is the story *not supposed to end*, but *it does not end*. Our experience in this world is merely the Introduction to the story. Chapter 1 of the story begins in eternity. However, while the story does not have an end, the good news is that suffering *does* have an end for those who believe in Jesus Christ.

As we've read so far, suffering in all its varied hues is a painful experience caused by sin in this world. Even people who know how to rightly respond to and endure suffering in the ways we've discussed still long for suffering to end. In this context, "endurance" is an interesting word, because inherent in the idea of enduring suffering is the promise that there is an end to it. In fact, you'll notice that the word "endurance" begins with the letters e-n-d. So for those who speak English it serves as an encouraging reminder that suffering does have an "end."

Just as suffering will have an end, endurance too will have an end. It will not last for eternity. In Heaven there will be no need to endure, because there will be no suffering for its citizens to experience. There will be no suffering in Heaven because there will be no sin, sinners, or sinfulness there. Absent sin, absent the need to endure suffering.

In Heaven, endurance experts will cross the finish line of the marathon of the Christian life to be greeted by our Savior, Jesus Christ, and a whole host of other endurance experts who ran before us. That's why the Bible reminds those of us who are running the race of endurance now,

> Therefore, since we have so great a cloud of witnesses surrounding us, let us also lay aside every encumbrance and the sin which so easily entangles us, and let us run with endurance the race that is set before us, fixing our eyes on Jesus, the author and perfecter of faith, who for the joy set before him endured the cross, despising the shame, and has sat down at the right hand of the throne of God. (Hebrews 12:1–2)

The "great cloud of witnesses" referred to here is composed of past endurance experts—all those believers in the Lord Jesus Christ who have suffered, endured, and gone on to be in the presence of God. Heaven is where all those endurance experts are. One day we will meet them. There is more I must write about Heaven, but before I do, we need a few reminders.

Seven Reminders that This World is Not Heaven

Writing in the historical context of World War II—when some people believed it was possible to have some kind of heaven on earth—C.S. Lewis said,

> A Christian cannot . . . believe any of those who promise that if only some reform in our economic, political, or hygienic system were made, a heaven on earth would follow . . . If applied to individual life, the doctrine that an imagined heaven on earth is necessary for vigorous attempts to remove present evil, would at once reveal its absurdity. Hungry men seek food and sick men healing none the less because they know after the meal or the cure, the ordinary ups and downs of life still await them.[80]

80. Lewis, *The Problem of Pain*, 115.

The End of Suffering

Today there are still hungry men who seek food and sick men who seek healing. So if we are wise, we will agree with Lewis and concede that while Heaven is for real, this present world clearly is not Heaven. If we think we can create heaven on earth, we may in the attempt end up creating a hell of sorts. As Lewis points out, "A Christian cannot . . . believe any of those who promise" that a heaven on earth is possible through the ingenuity of man. It's just absurd. I want to highlight seven realities (among many others) which stand as reminders that this present world is not Heaven, nor ever can be.

Poverty

There are parts of the world today that seem heaven-like, evoking expressions like "It's like being in heaven here" because of some natural beauty or manmade opulence. But amid beauty and opulence is the ever-lingering problem of poverty. Some people lack the most basic material and financial necessities of life. Jesus said, "For you always have the poor with you" (Mark 14:7). He was using the "always," of course, to refer to the temporary duration for which this world of suffering and sin will last—until we're in Heaven. As Jesus said, today we still have the poor with us. Every nation, every city, has its poor and destitute, and poverty is surely a cause of suffering.

The "American dream"—job security, raises in pay, a house, a family, cars, insurance(s), vacations, etcetera—is a goal towards which many people have worked. For some, the dream has been realized with material and financial prosperity. For others, however, the dream will never be realized. Also, pursuing the American dream has not been able so far to fully remove poverty and the suffering that comes with it. The United States Census Bureau reports that in 2017, there were 39.7 million people living in poverty.[81] In Heaven, however, poverty will be removed, and something far greater than the American dream will become a reality for those who trust in Jesus. It is good for us to work to alleviate poverty, because God in Christ has shown us mercy and so should we to those in need—but until there is absolutely no poverty to alleviate, be assured we are not in Heaven.

---

81. Fontenot, Semega, and Kollar, "Income and Poverty in the United States."

Predation

Predators in this fallen world are another cause of suffering. Animal predators prey on weaker animals, and attack and kill humans even as of 2018![82] But worse, there are human predators— sexual predators who prey on victims and steal a part of someone's life. The suffering caused by rape, incest, molestation, or any other form of predation is reported every day in the news. TIME magazine recently reported a shocking case in Liberia, where the co-founder of an organization that rescued young girls from sex trafficking was himself preying on the girls who were rescued. He was raping those who had been brought to the organization's building for refuge.[83] Such predatorial acts in supposed safe-havens only confirm that we are not in Heaven. In Heaven, there will be no predators of any kind.

Pain: Physical, Emotional, Social

Sometimes when I hear sirens blaring in Chicago (which is very often), I think to myself, "That's the sound of suffering," an auditory symbol of pain in this world. The ambulance rushes with its sirens to attend to someone who is in physical pain. The police car cuts through downtown traffic with lights flashing, meaning a perpetrator is being, or will be, apprehended for some crime committed and there will be pain of all kinds. The fire truck reminds us with its siren that fire destroys life and property and causes pain. As long as you hear the sound of sirens, you hear the sound of suffering and pain, and should be reminded this world is not Heaven. In Heaven, pain will not be a problem any longer, and we will hear no sirens there.

A Peaceless Globe

As we near the end of November 2018, even as I write, the Council on Foreign Relations reports a grim picture of the state of the world through its Global Conflict Tracker.[84] We live in a peaceless world in which nations are at war and in conflict with each other. To name just a few, there's the North Korea crisis, war in Afghanistan, civil war in Syria, the Israel-Palestinian conflict, Boko Haram in Nigeria, and conflict between India and Pakistan.

---

82. Elsevier, "Number of people killed by animals."
83. Vick, "Hidden in Plain Sight," Time Magazine 64–5
84. Council on Foreign Relations, "Global Conflict Tracker."

The United Nations may try to bring peace to this globe, but ultimately it cannot bring lasting peace. How can anyone think that such a war-torn world is Heaven, or that Heaven is possible in such a world? In Heaven, there will be no war or conflict.

Persecution

In October 2018, Pastor Andrew Brunson was released by Turkey after having been held in prison for a year and a half. Pastor Andrew served the people of Turkey, preaching Jesus Christ for 23 years, only to be falsely accused of terrorism. In an interview with an American news channel after being released, Pastor Andrew said that during his time in prison he began to lose hope. However, he explained, God helped him.

> I began to see that there was value in my suffering, especially as time went on. I saw that many people around the world began praying for me. And I began to see that God was involved in this ... and that God was going to do something with my suffering that had value.[85]

God is involved in the suffering of all his children, and while we rejoice at the release of Pastor Andrew, not everyone who suffers for the sake of Jesus Christ makes it through persecution alive. Thousands upon thousands of Christians are being persecuted all over the world right now, by people who hate them simply because they are Christian. Jesus promised his followers that we would have persecution on this side of eternity. If you are a Christian, pray for and weep with your persecuted brothers and sisters. People are also persecuted in the name of ethnic cleansing. I am thinking of the Rohingya crisis in Myanmar. On the other side of the finish line, in Heaven, there will be no persecution, either of Christians nor of any other people. Until then, however, persecution is another reminder we are not in Heaven.

Prejudice

If there ever was a time when racial tension and ethnic prejudices seemed like they were at an all-time high, it is now. In a nation whose currency reads *E Pluribus Unum*—"out of the many, one"—instances of ethnic prejudice

---

85. Fox News, "Sean Hannity Interviews Pastor Brunson."

are common. On one hand you have the Black Lives Matter movement that has garnered momentum because of what some perceive as unjust "white privilege" asserting itself in the U.S. On the other hand, you have various White Supremacist movements. Both extremes are certainly prejudiced, wrong, and unchristian. All lives matter! And only Christ is to be supreme in our lives! Where does one find middle ground? In the Church? Even the evangelical Church in America can sometimes be ethnically prejudiced.

I believe there are two tests for racism or ethnocentrism in the heart of a Christian: marriage and ministry. Do we embrace *inter-ethnic marriage between Christians*? And do we submit to the *spiritual authority of someone from another ethnicity*, especially if they are not from the dominant ethnicity, for fear of our ethnicity losing control or power? These are not simple or easy-to-answer questions. You say, "Give me a real-life illustration that this exists in the Church." I could give you many, but I choose not to. Go search your own heart and church to see if ethnic prejudice exists or not. Sadly, in many pockets of the Church we find that it still does. In Heaven this will not be the case. But for now, ethnic prejudice is a reminder we are not in Heaven.

Partisan Politics

The party system is one of the beauties—and at the same time one of the horrors—of democracy. Today, thanks to the media, the contrast and divide between Republican and Democratic supporters in the U.S. is even more sharply felt than before. This tension is sometimes felt most palpably in the evangelical Church. We can sometimes be a politically divided bunch. In the U.S., we get to vote. We have our rights and choices for parties and Presidents. But in Heaven there will be no choice, and no vote about who rules! Until then, partisan politics and the resulting great divide are a constant reminder we are not in Heaven.

Hell: Eternal Regret

Why write about Hell after being reminded that this world is not Heaven? Mainly because it is a biblical doctrine and the other half of the truth. If Heaven is one half of the truth about our eternal destiny—that time and place with no suffering—then Hell is the other half of the truth—that time and place with unending suffering. In answering the question "Will there be an end to all suffering?" I wish I could say there will be an end to *all* suffering. As I was contemplating a title for this chapter, I was thinking of adding the world "all" to the title "The End of Suffering." However, I cannot use "all," lest I propagate a lie. All suffering will end for those who are in Heaven, true. But not all suffering in the universe will end. Those outside Heaven, out of Christ and apart from God, will be plunged into an eternity of immeasurable and unending suffering. The Bible calls the place of this eternal suffering Hell.

In Hell, the seven present reminders that this world is not Heaven will become eternal regrets. Moreover, all these realities will be perpetually magnified. In Hell, people will be *poverty* stricken forever, with no charity to help; *predators* will prey eternally on the inhabitants of Hell; *pain* of all kinds will gnaw at body, soul, and mind; the *peaceless* state of hearts will get worse every day, never to be calmed; unrepentant *persecutors* on earth will become the persecuted and tormented; everyone will be *prejudiced* against everyone else for every reason possible, as hate will be the norm; *partisanship* will rule as people will forever be divided, and unable to ever unite to get themselves out of Hell.

Besides these, there will be innumerably more earthly vices that will be magnified in Hell, as people pine away and suffer forever. That's why the Bible says of the inhabitants of Hell, "And the smoke of their torment goes up forever and ever; they have no rest day and night. . ." (Revelation 14:11). There is never rest in Hell, only eternal regret, remorse, and retribution. Be warned of Hell and rush to Christ today if you have never done so. Trust him to save you from your sin and from eternal suffering. Christ alone can grant you eternal life and entry into Heaven.

Heaven: Eternal Rewards

Finally! . . . You have reached the end of the marathon race of suffering in life. You cross the finish line and run through the tape. As soon as you break through the tape, you are transformed totally, the world around you morphs instantly, and everyone around you is different. The light is suddenly unalloyed purity. The air is literally celestial. And the dread weight you were carrying all your life—that weight which owed its existence to the reason for suffering in the world, sin—is gone. You are in Heaven. You have arrived. There stands the Lord Jesus Christ. He receives your hand from your angel escort, embraces you, and says, "Welcome home, child of God!"

No wonder the God of the Bible does not allow us to settle down here in this world, as if Heaven on earth were possible or as if this were our home. The welcome by Jesus himself, and everything that follows it eternally, will be worth the wait. C.S. Lewis said,

> Our Father refreshes us on the journey with some pleasant inns, but will not encourage us to mistake them for home. [86]

The "pleasant inns" on earth are but reminders of the home Jesus has gone to prepare for us; none of them are our final home. The problem is, many people do mistake the pleasant inns as their final home because of the great amount of patience and endurance required in suffering as we wait for Heaven. The long haul of the wait, coupled with nothing seeming to happen for the present—that is, none of the eschatological claims of Christ seeming to come to pass—is what induces a spirit of unbelief and a hardness of heart in many people. The late Australian atheist J.L. Mackie once quipped,

> If the theists tell us that God will eventually bring this utopia into being, the critics can hardly be blamed for wondering why he has gone such a long way round about it.[87]

Why indeed has God gone "such a long way round about it?" If Mr. Mackie were alive today, we might have replied, "Yes, God has gone a long way round about it—from *our* perspective, that is. But eternity will be even longer. This life is a dot at the beginning of the line which stretches on for infinity. Besides, things of 'lasting' value on earth, such as great pieces of art or magnificent buildings, take a long time to create or build, don't they? Why should we be surprised that God is taking his 'time' to build our homes in Heaven which will last for eternity?" Whether or not that answer would have convinced Mr. Mackie, I don't know. But if you have no hope of Heaven, or if you don't believe in the God who has promised Heaven to those who believe in Jesus, I hope this helps convince you to get one step closer to trusting in Jesus Christ. The reality is that there is a lifetime involved in waiting for Heaven. But Jesus has promised,

> "In My Father's house are many dwelling places; if it were not so, I would have told you; for I go to prepare a place for you. If I go and prepare a place for you, I will come again and

---

86. Lewis, *The Problem of Pain*, 116.
87. Jones, *Why Does God Allow Evil*, 181.

receive you to Myself, that where I am, there you may be also." (John 14:2–3)

Jesus has gone to prepare a place for us, a home in Heaven. The time between when he ascended into Heaven after his resurrection, and his return to take his followers to be with him, is the time of his preparing this promised home in Heaven, which is only one of the many eternal rewards we will receive. What are some of the other rewards that endurance experts who suffered according to God's plan will receive in Heaven as part of this home?

The Reversal of the Seven Reminders

Among a whole host of other things, in Heaven God will reverse the seven realities which are reminders that this present world is not Heaven.

In Heaven, the *poverty* of the children of God will be reversed to *riches*. We will be richer than any prosperity gospel preacher's wildest imagination. Jesus said, "Do not fear, little flock, for it is your Father's good pleasure to give you the kingdom" (Luke 12:32, NKJV). If we who endure suffering on earth are given the very kingdom of God in Heaven, that says enough of how rich we already are! There is no place for poverty in Heaven for children of the King! Neither is there any place for *predation* in Heaven. The Bible says, "And the wolf will dwell with the lamb, and the leopard will lie down with the young goat, and the calf and the young lion and the fatling together; and a little boy will lead them . . . They will not hurt or destroy in all My holy mountain" (Isaiah 11:6–9). No animal predators will be present; neither will human predators who commit egregious acts of immorality, because as the Bible says, "But for the cowardly and unbelieving and abominable and murderers and immoral persons . . . their part will be in the lake that burns with fire and brimstone" (Revelation 21:8).

In Heaven, all *pain* will be reversed to *comfort and pleasure*. The problem of pain will be dealt with decisively, once and for all. The Bible says that in Heaven, God "will wipe away every tear from their eyes; and there will no longer be any death; there will no longer be any mourning, or crying, or pain; the first things have passed away" (Revelation 21:4). Not only will all pain be wiped away, but this *peaceless state* we are in will be forever transformed into a state of *perfect and lasting peace*. The Bible calls Jesus Christ the Prince of Peace, and when he establishes his rule, "There will be no end to the increase of his government or of peace" (Isaiah 9:7).

Moreover, under the government of Jesus, the *persecution* his followers underwent on earth will be *finally vindicated*. The book of Revelation describes the cry of justice that comes from the souls of those who are martyred for the sake of Jesus Christ: " . . . and they cried out with a loud voice, saying, 'How long, O Lord, holy and true, will You refrain from judging and avenging our blood on those who dwell on the earth?'" (Revelation 6:10). God answers that cry for justice a little later in the book of Revelation, as the entire world system which persecutes Christians—depicted as the whore of Babylon—is judged by God because she "was corrupting the earth with her immorality, and he has avenged the blood of his bond-servants on her" (Revelation 19:2). Justice will finally be served and everyone who *ever* persecuted Christians without repenting (including the Devil, according to Revelation 20:10) will receive their just desserts, forever.

In Heaven, *racial and ethnic prejudices* will be reversed *to interethnic harmony and love*. The Bible says, "After these things I looked, and behold, a great multitude which no one could count, from every nation and all tribes and peoples and tongues, standing before the throne and before the Lamb" (Revelation 7:9). Every people group and ethnicity and nation will be represented in Heaven. We will all be united in love, while yet retaining our uniqueness. Further, the Bible says, "they will bring the glory and the honor of the nations into it" (Revelation 21:26). All the deplorable aspects of every ethnicity and culture will be excluded from Heaven. Only the glorious and honorable aspects will be allowed, thus making us appreciate and love cultures other than our own like never before.

Lastly, in Heaven partisanship will be impossible. We will have a perfectly unified front with regard to who is in power over us. In fact, the reason such unity and love among ethnicities will be possible in Heaven is because of who will be ruling as the Head of all these nations and peoples. Before the eternal kingdom in Heaven, there will be period of a thousand years when Jesus rules on the earth visibly and physically. The Bible says of this time, "From his mouth comes a sharp sword, so that with it he may strike down the nations, and he will rule them with a rod of iron" (Revelation 19:15). During this time, people will still desire to usurp authority and form political parties against the rule of Jesus. But he will rule with "a rod of iron"—with such irresistible power and justice that none shall be able to usurp political authority. In Heaven, however, when Jesus Christ rules everyone, the sinful desire to usurp authority will be absent since sin will be absent. There will therefore be no need to ever vote again in Heaven.

The End of Suffering

The Overturning of the Reason for Suffering

In Chapter 5 we explored extensively the reason for suffering in general, which is sin. We learned that "the whole creation groans and suffers the pains of childbirth together until now," and that "the creation was subjected to futility, not willingly, but because of him who subjected it, in hope that the creation itself also will be set free from its slavery to corruption into the freedom of the glory of the children of God" (Romans 8:20–22). In Heaven, the creation that was enslaved to transience because of sin is restored to the original freedom and permanence it had before the Fall. The Bible says, "Then I saw a new heaven and a new earth; for the first heaven and the first earth passed away" (Revelation 21:1). All of creation is made new because there is no sin. And when there is no sin, God's curse that enslaved creation (recorded in Genesis 3), subjecting it to futility, will be lifted. The Bible says, "There will no longer be any curse; and the throne of God and of the Lamb will be in it" (Revelation 22:3).

The Reward of All Rewards

Besides all that I've mentioned here, there will be many untold rewards in Heaven for endurance experts who suffered on earth. But all of them will pale into insignificance compared to the greatest of all rewards we will receive. Nothing will compare to the reward of having God himself: being with him, seeing him face to face, knowing him like never before, unhindered by our sinful constitutions and dispositions.

Please never forget: God himself is and will be our greatest reward. The extent to which we are satisfied with this Reward of rewards is a good indicator of one's spiritual maturity and ability to endure suffering well.

From Genesis to Revelation, the great theme of the Bible is that the almighty and infinite God pledges himself as the reward of his people. In Genesis the Lord promised Abraham, "I am thy shield, and thy exceeding great reward" (Genesis 15:1, KJV). The Bible ends with, "And I heard a great voice out of heaven saying, 'Behold, the tabernacle of God is with men, and he will dwell with them, and they shall be his people, and God himself shall be with them, and be their God'" (Revelation 21:3). This is why we endure suffering and do not escape, because after this life is done and God brings us to Heaven, we will be with God himself. All the suffering we faced on earth will pale into oblivion in light of the sheer pleasure and awe of being with Jesus Christ himself, forever.

Finally, in the presence of God, there will be one more notable reward Heaven offers us. In conclusion, I would like to dwell on this reward as we tie this book together.

The End of Suffering: When East and West Converge

In explaining what I mean by the convergence of East and West in Heaven, I should reiterate my viewpoint in writing (also the subtitle of this book): namely, that I have attempted this work from the viewpoint of *an Eastern Millennial living in the West*.

As I scour the sweep of world history and find myself living in this global village today, I am convinced that the West has profound lessons to offer the East, and the East has profound lessons to offer the West. It is never a one-way street. Easterners help Westerners see their blind spots, and Westerners help Easterners see theirs. In so doing, we are able to see beyond an Eastern or Western viewpoint and therefore see the world more wholly, especially in the context of rightly responding to suffering. We have seen some of this from discussions in the preceding chapters, but we have just scratched the surface. There is much for us to learn about how people in the *other* hemisphere approach the problem of pain and suffering. In his book *Why Suffering?* Ravi Zacharias offers this helpful framework of differences for how the East and West tackle the question of suffering,

> In the West, the difficulty behind the question is juxtaposing overall purpose and love . . . the mitigation of pain in the physical world is seen as an advance, but the spiritual strength that enables a person to persevere in the face of pain is considered unreal and belittled.[88]

> In the East, the problem is stated so that the focus is on the cause of a specific suffering and how to eliminate it . . . rather than seeking to bring physical relief, [it] is either totally spiritualized or used to develop a philosophy . . . it is not the question to the existence of God that is raised but . . . the why of it all.[89]

---

88. Zacharias and Vitale, *Why Suffering*, 113–4.
89. Zacharias and Vitale, *Why Suffering*, 113–5.

The End of Suffering

The West looks to answer *how to mitigate pain in suffering*. The East looks to answer *why there is suffering*. But we need to know the *why* before we can answer the *how*, and without the *how*, the *why* is practically meaningless. We need both why and how. We need Eastern *and* Western perspectives. This ability today to view the world more readily and accessibly through a composite East-West lens is one of the greatest marvels of our global village, in my humble opinion.

But then I think of how these East-West worldview relationships began prior to the global village. For instance, take the history of the spread of the gospel in the three centuries preceding the global village phenomenon: how Western missionaries felt called to bring the light of the gospel to Eastern lands. Christians in the East, for example in India, are indebted to the efforts of William Carey, the pioneer British missionary who lived in India. With his eighteenth and nineteenth-century Western worldview, Carey lived as an Easterner; he lived as an Indian helping Hindus see the darkness of the caste system and the horror of Sati (widow burning) by shining the light of the gospel into their lives. It amazes me that the spirit of these Eastern religions—which Carey and later British and American missionaries sought to rescue people from—has today sprung up in the very lands these missionaries hailed from, plunging so many Westerners into darkness.

Is it not incumbent then upon Eastern missionaries now to shine that same gospel light here in the West? To warn Westerners that the very spiritual influences which bound our ancestors in the East are here to bind this generation and the coming ones? Among other things, please treat what I have written in this book (especially in Chapters 1, 3, and 4) as that warning or plea from an Eastern missionary in the West, one who is attempting to expose certain dark Eastern spiritual influences that are eroding the great Judeo-Christian theme of endurance in suffering. Without endurance in suffering, the Christian life, the Church, and Judeo-Christian convictions are impossible to sustain. I'm not the only Easterner living in the West who is concerned. Ravi Zacharias relates the views of a former Muslim, now a Christian, on faith and conviction in the West today. Ravi explains,

> He drew two circles and put a small dot in each of them. Pointing to the first he said, 'As a Muslim I believed the circle to be my faith, and the little dot to be my life.' Then he pointed to the next circle and said, 'Now, as a follower of Jesus, I have seen the difference in

cultural tension. To many Westerners, the circle is his life and the dot his faith.' . . .

'That is why,' he added, 'the West will ultimately be overrun. Faith, in the West, is a kind of extracurricular interest and a mere aspect of life for the sake of inner peace. But faith seldom enters the mind as a conviction.'[90]

Of course, the man in the illustration is speaking of non-Christian Westerners, because for true Christians our faith is the circle and our life the dot. Nonetheless, it is a helpful question to ask both Christians and non-Christians: which one is your life, and which one is your faith? And if you are Christian, do you still hold your faith as a conviction, or is it a matter of convenience? If faith is a conviction of the heart and mind for you, so will endurance be. If not, convenience will be the name of the game, and if that's the case for the majority of the West, then yes, "the West [as we know it] will ultimately be overrun."

My point in discussing how East and West help each other view the world more holistically is to say that *a humble posture of learning* from people of the West (if you are from the East), or from people of the East (if you are from the West), *is a preview of Heaven,* where all suffering will end. For in Heaven, these East-West divergences that separate us on earth will converge perfectly to unite us. This convergence of the East and West is possible only in Christ, and on earth we see a dim but powerful preview of it in the Church of Christ.

William Dunkerly wrote the words to the hymn "In Christ There Is No East or West," inspired by Rudyard Kipling's famed "Ballad of the East and West." Kipling's view was,

> Oh, East is East, and West is West, and never the twain shall meet,
> Till Earth and Sky stand presently at God's great Judgment Seat.

Dunkerly expanded on Kipling's view and wrote,

> Join hands, then, members of the faith,
> Whatever your race may be!
> Who serves my Father as his child
> Is surely kin to me.

---

90. Zacharias and Vitale, *Jesus among Secular gods,* 11.

The End of Suffering

> In Christ now meet both East and West,
> In him meet North and South;
> All Christly souls are one in him
> Throughout the whole wide earth.

Yes, East and West will converge perfectly only in Heaven; but in Christ, people of the East and West meet today in a spiritual union that can only be experienced and understood by one who has believed in the person and work of Jesus Christ. Ask any Christian from any nation—even when we cannot speak the same language, as fellow believers in each other's presence, there is an otherworldly attraction and love for each other that transcends the East-West divide.

Since suffering will end in Heaven where East and West perfectly converge, then we would do well now to learn about responding to suffering biblically from the imperfect convergence and even divergence of East and West. What does that mean practically, though? Let me offer three suggestions, please.

1. Look to begin an in-person friendship with someone from the other hemisphere (preferably of the same gender), to learn from them as you get to know them in their own suffering.
2. If possible, consider taking a trip to the other hemisphere to learn firsthand how people of those cultures respond to suffering, and how it fits (or doesn't) with the Christian, biblical responses expressed here.
3. If the first two suggestions are not possible, connect with someone from the other hemisphere on social media. Correspond with them about these issues, exchanging East-West viewpoints, again seeing whether what you learn fits with the Christian, biblical responses.

What are the benefits to following these suggestions? For one, these steps will expand our worldview and take us out of our comfort zone, which is a good place from which to begin learning how to rightly respond to suffering. Two, these steps will help us respond more biblically and faithfully to suffering by seeing how our brothers and sisters all over the world endure suffering biblically. Three, these steps will prepare us for Heaven, where we will be with those brothers and sisters from all over the world, when none of us will have to endure suffering anymore.

While *enduring suffering* may be learned from an Eastern or Western biblical viewpoint, in the end, *escaping suffering* on our own will be proven to be *not* a matter of East or West, but a matter of one single direction in which all rebellious humans travel: away from God. It is this God people run away from today who will be celebrated in Heaven, when East and West converge and men and women gather from across time, from every location and direction on earth. In Heaven, God will prove he is the Father of us all—the Father who allows us to suffer for a little while to teach us and complete us, but then gives us eternal joy and pleasure in his presence.

Epilogue

When God Gives Out the Medals

CONSIDER AGAIN THE LAST words of the Buddha from Chapter 1:

> The master opened his lips a last time, 'All things individual die—strive earnestly—to find liberation—' his last faint words mingled and were lost in the breeze that stirred the sal trees.[91]

Oh! the ring of hopelessness in these last words from the so-called enlightened one. What light or hope do these words give a suffering person? Now contrast the last words of a dying Buddha with the last words of the risen Christ on earth—the Christ who was crucified, died, and was buried, but rose again on the third day:

> "All authority has been given to Me in heaven and on earth. Go therefore and make disciples of all the nations, baptizing them in the name of the Father and the Son and the Holy Spirit, teaching them to observe all that I commanded you; and lo, I am with you always, even to the end of the age." (Matthew 28:18–20)

Having risen from the dead, notice in Jesus' words the phrases "all authority," "all nations," "all that I commanded you," and "with you always" (literally all the days), till "the end" of this age. When this age ends, when Christ pronounces the grand "The End" which we have been waiting for, suffering will end, and eternity will only begin to begin in Heaven. Jesus Christ is with us to the end, and when that end comes, we'll be with him without end.

91. Byles, *Footprints of the Gautama Buddha*, 204–5.

Endurance Experts

This year (2018), the Chicago Marathon was held in overcast conditions. I had the opportunity to stand on the sidelines again to watch and cheer the athletes as they passed by, flint-faced, having just one goal in mind: beginning mile 1, and finishing mile 26.2. What went on between these mile markers was endurance. This year's Marathon was won by Mo Farah, a British Olympic gold medalist in 2012 and 2016 in both the 5,000- and 10,000-meter races. When Farah and every other runner who followed him crossed the finish line, they received a medal, a tangible recognition that they had endured and finished the race. Their medals make me hearken back to 22-year-old Eric Liddell's comments when he became the 1924 Scottish Olympic hero, winning gold for the 400 meters:

> It has been wonderful to compete in the Olympic Games and to bring home a gold medal. But since I have been a young lad, I have had my eyes on a different prize. You see, each of us is in a greater race than any I have run in Paris, and this race ends when God gives out the medals.[92]

I'm sure when Liddell crossed the finish line into eternity, the Lord Jesus welcomed him with open arms. Whether he has received his medal yet or not, I'm certain he'll be part of a future prize ceremony in which all endurance experts will be rewarded. I hope to so run that by God's grace I endure—having my eyes, like Liddell's, on a "different prize."

Thank you for joining me on this journey to becoming an endurance expert. I hope and pray that what you read has helped or will help you in some measure to respond rightly to suffering and to cross the finish line into eternity. I pray I see you on the other side of the finish line, *"when God gives out the medals."*

The End . . . of this book!

---

92. Benge, *Eric Liddell*, 69.

Bibliography

Benge, Janet and Geoff. *Eric Liddell: Something Greater than Gold.* Seattle: YWAM, 1998.
Buddhanet (website). "Life of the Buddha (part 2)." 2008. Accessed December 7, 2018. www.buddhanet.net/e-learning/buddhism/lifebuddha/2_31lbud.htm
Bullock, Alan. *Hitler: A Study in Tyranny.* New York: HarperCollins, 1971.
Byles, Marie Beuzeville. *Footprints of the Gautama Buddha.* Wheaton: Theosophical, 1967.
Chesterton, G.K. *Orthodoxy.* Colorado Springs: Harold Shaw, 2001.
Connor, Steve. "The People Who Can't Feel Pain." *The Independent.* May 25, 2015. Accessed December 7, 2018. www.independent.co.uk/life-style/health-and-families/health-news/the-people-who-cant-feel-pain-scientists-discover-cause-of-rare-inherited-condition-that-turns-off-10274604.html
Cowman, Mrs. Charles. "Made Perfect Through Suffering." *Back to the Bible.* Accessed December 7, 2018. www.backtothebible.org/devotions/made-perfect-through-suffering
Dawkins, Richard. *A River Out of Eden.* New York: HarperCollins, 1995.
Diamond, Stephen. "Anger and Catharsis: Myth, Metaphor or Reality?" *Psychology Today.* September 30, 2009. Accessed December 7, 2018. www.psychologytoday.com/blog/evil-deeds/200909/anger-and-catharsis-myth-metaphor-or-reality
Drummond, Richard H. *Gautama the Buddha.* Grand Rapids: Eerdmans, 1974.
Elsevier, website. "Number of people killed by animals each year in the US remains unchanged." February 28, 2018. Accessed December 7, 2018. www.elsevier.com/about/press-releases/research-and-journals/number-of-people-killed-by-animals-each-year-in-the-us-remains-unchanged
Fontenot, Kayla, Jessica Semega, and Melissa Kollar. "Income and Poverty in the United States." *United States Census Bureau.* September 12, 2018. Accessed December 7, 2018. www.census.gov/library/publications/2018/demo/p60-263.html
FoxNews. "Sean Hannity interviews Pastor Andrew Brunson." YouTube video, 4:56. October 16, 2018. www.youtube.com/watch?v=XWviGuY0-4c
Global Conflict Tracker. Council on Foreign Relations. December 7, 2018. Accessed December 7, 2018. www.cfr.org/interactives/global-conflict-tracker#!/global-conflict-tracker
Hill, Jonathan. *The History of Christianity.* Grand Rapids: Zondervan, 2006.
Holocombe, Kate. "Reduce Suffering: How Yoga Heals." *Yoga Journal.* October 10, 2013. Accessed December 7, 2018. www.yogajournal.com/yoga-101/ultimate-practice

Bibliography

I Commit to Pray (website). "Church Disbands Because of Hindu Persecution." December 6, 2018. Accessed December 7, 2018. www.icommittopray.com/request/1802/pakhluwa-church-members/

Jayaram, V. "The Definition and Concept of Maya in Hinduism." *Hindu Website*. Accessed December 7, 2018. www.hinduwebsite.com/hinduism/essays/maya.asp

Jones, Clay. *Why Does God Allow Evil?* Eugene, OR: Harvest House, 2017.

Keller, Timothy. *The Reason for God*. New York: Riverhead, 2008.

Lewis, C.S. *The Problem of Pain*. New York: HarperCollins, 2001.

Longerich, Peter. "The Nazi Racial State." *The BBC*. Feb 17, 2011. Accessed December 7, 2018. www.bbc.co.uk/history/worldwars/genocide/racial_state_01.shtml

Louw, J.P. and E.A. Nida. *Greek-English Lexicon of the New Testament: Based on Semantic Domains*. 2nd edition, Vol. 1. New York: United Bible Societies, 1996. Logos Bible Software.

Lutzer, Erwin. *Christ Among Other gods: A Defense of Christ in an Age of Tolerance*. Chicago: Moody, 1994.

———. *Hitler's Cross*. Chicago: Moody, 1995.

MacArthur, John. *The MacArthur New Testament Commentary: James*. Chicago: Moody, 1998.

MacDonald George. *Unspoken Sermons*. London: Alexander Strahan, 1867.

Merriam-Webster's Collegiate Dictionary (11th ed.). (2003). Springfield, MA: Merriam-Webster Incorporated.

Newton, Isaac. *The Mathematical Principles of Natural Philosophy*. Translated by Andrew Motte. New York: George Putnam, 1850.

Osteen, Joel. *Your Best Life Now*. New York: Warner Faith, 2014.

Peale, Norman Vincent. *The Power of Positive Thinking*. New York: Simon and Schuster, 1952.

Phillips, Richard. *The Story of Gautama Buddha and His Creed: An Epic*. London: Longmans Green, 1871.

Prisoner Alert (website), a Ministry of Voice of the Martyrs. Accessed December 7, 2018. www.prisoneralert.com/vompw_prisoners.html

Quinn, William Wilson. "What's an American Buddhist?" *OnFaith* (originally published for *The Washington Post*). June 17, 2012. Accessed December 7, 2018. www.onfaith.co/onfaith/2012/06/17/whats-an-american-buddhist/10071

Schmutzer, Andrew and Gerald Peterman. *Between Pain and Grace*. Chicago: Moody, 2016.

Solzhenitsyn, Aleksandr I. *The Gulag Archipelago: 1918–1956*. New York: Harper and Row, 1973.

Stewart, James S. *The Strong Name*. Edinburgh: T. & T. Clark, 1940.

The Heart of Hinduism, website. "Maya: Illusion." Accessed December 7, 2018. iskconeducationalservices.org/HoH/concepts/105.htm

TheKbeal. "Hitler's Utopia-Power." YouTube video, 5:33. October 28, 2012. www.youtube.com/watch?v=7iSxbmkKQMk

Veith, Gene Edward, Jr. *Post Modern Times: A Christian Guide to Contemporary Thought and Culture*. Wheaton: Crossway, 1994.

Vick, Karl. "Hidden in Plain Sight." TIME magazine, November 5, 2018.

Warfield, B.B. *The Person and Work of Christ*. Philadelphia: Presbyterian and Reformed, 1970.

Wiersbe, W.W. *Be Available*. Wheaton: Victor, 1994.

Bibliography

———. *The Bible Exposition Commentary,* Vol. 2. Wheaton: Victor, 1996.

Winfrey, Oprah. "What Oprah Knows for Sure about Finding Hope and Peace." *Oprah.com.* May 2018. Accessed December 7, 2018. www.oprah.com/inspiration/oprah-on-hope-and-peace

Wootson Jr., Cleve R. "A televangelist wants his followers to pay for a $54 million private jet. It's his fourth plane." *The Washington Post.* May 29, 2018. Accessed December 7, 2018. www.washingtonpost.com/news/acts-of-faith/wp/2018/05/29/a-televangelist-wants-his-followers-to-pay-for-a-54-million-private-jet-its-his-fourth-plane

Wuthnow, Robert. *After the Baby Boomers: How Twenty-and-Thirty-Somethings are Shaping the Future of American Religion.* Princeton: Princeton University Press, 2010.

Zacharias, Ravi. *The End of Reason.* Grand Rapids: Zondervan, 2008.

Zacharias, Ravi and Vince Vitale. *Jesus among Secular gods: The Countercultural Claims of Christ.* New York: Faith Words, 2017.

———. *Why Suffering: Finding Meaning and Comfort When Life Doesn't Make Sense.* New York: Faith Words, 2014.

Also by Kenny Damara

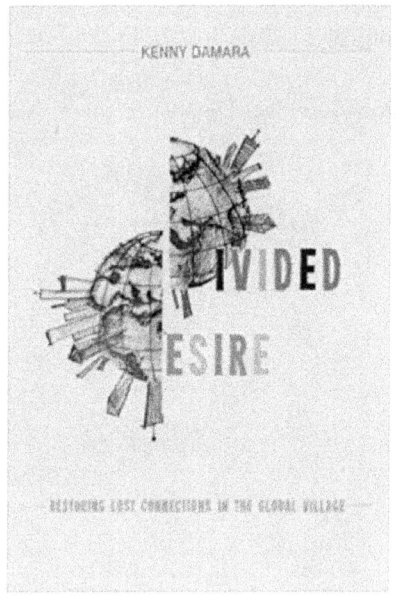

*Divided Desire:
Restoring Lost Connections in the Global Village*

Everywhere you look, every time you listen, and with each click, there's some-thing you desire. The global village presents innumerable ways to connect to information. We think we can scarcely live without these connections but sometimes we do not realize that connections from the media block or slow down connections to God, self, and others. How do these connections influence the desires of your heart?

What role does God have in helping you fulfill your ultimate desire?

In *Divided Desire* Kenny Damara explores questions about why we desire what we desire today, and how we can find satisfaction.

"This book analyzes our desires which are often deeply buried within us, and which we need to acknowledge and direct godward. Kenny shows us the importance of our desires and how they can be managed for the glory of God."

—ERWIN LUTZER, PASTOR EMERITUS,
THE MOODY CHURCH

PURCHASE YOUR COPY ONLINE AT:

https://wipfandstock.com/divided-desire.html

https://www.amazon.com/Divided-Desire-Restoring-Connections-Village/dp/1625642113

www.ingramcontent.com/pod-product-compliance
Lightning Source LLC
Chambersburg PA
CBHW070928160426
43193CB00011B/1615